Research Guide to Loyalist Ancestors

A Directory to Archives, Manuscripts, Published and Electronic Sources

(Updated and Revised)

Paul J. Bunnell, F.A.C.G., U.E.

HERITAGE BOOKS
2006

HERITAGE BOOKS
AN IMPRINT OF HERITAGE BOOKS, INC.

Books, CDs, and more—Worldwide

For our listing of thousands of titles see our website
at
www.HeritageBooks.com

Published 2006 by
HERITAGE BOOKS, INC.
Publishing Division
65 East Main Street
Westminster, Maryland 21157-5026

International Standard Book Number: 978-0-7884-1425-9

This Book Is Dedicated To The Memory

Of

My Parents

James Henry Bunnell Sr.

and

Lorraine Muriel (Violette) Bunnell

and

Patricia D. (McCoy) White
(My mother-in-law)

Special Thanks To

Patricia D. (McCoy) White

and

Thomas R. Lynch R.Ph.

and

Greg M. Masterson
General Manager (1990) of the
Cape Cod Community College Library
West Barnstable, Massachusetts

Quote from a possible loyalist descendant

"So if you're lost and on your own;
You can never surrender;
And if your path won't lead you home;
You can never surrender.
"And when the night is cold and dark,
you can see; you can see light
cause no one can take your right to fight;
and to never surrender."

"Time is all we're looking for."

Words and song by
Cory Hart, Canadian Rock Artist

Special Thoughts To

Corporal & Farmer, Benjamin Bonnell/Bunnell, U.E.

(An American Loyalist)

(b.c. 1744 – d. 17 Feb. 1828)

Loyalist Refugee with his wife, Sarah (Sally) Jones and two children in 1779. Indicted for carrying counterfeit money for the British, fleeing New Jersey for New York City

Served under Brig. General Benedict Arnold's American Legion, August 1781 to c. 1783. Attacked the city New London and Fort Griswold, Connecticut 9 Sept. 1781 burning it to the ground in a very controversial battle. Also was listed in the Kings American Regiment c. 1783

Loyalist Refugee with family as passenger on the ship "William" in July 1783 from New York City to Saint John, Nova Scotia (New Brunswick), Canada

Grantee of ten acres of land (In Matthew Haines Land Grant with others) in 1784 living in what was called the "Tent City" of Saint John

One on the First Loyalist Settlers of Westfield (Long Reach), Kings County, New Brunswick, Canada, August 1786, 200 acres granted by King George III for service on the side of Great Britain

Table of Contents

Preface

There are many records scattered throughout the world regarding the American Loyalists. I have listed nearly all those locations, but unfortunately, many libraries and archives still hide much about these losers of the American Revolution. Without the help of societies such as The United Empire Loyalists' Association of Canada, and The Hereditary Order of Descendants of The Loyalists and Patriots of The American Revolution, and of the many loyalist descendants doing research, there would be no history preserved on the American Loyalists' today.

One highlight of my life was the meeting of His Royal Highness The Prince Philip at the UEL Convention in Lennoxville, Quebec in 1989. Later, he accepted my first book; "Thunder Over New England, Benjamin Bonnell, The Loyalist" which was placed in the Royal Library. A signed photo and letter from Buckingham Palace reminds me of that wonderful time.

Nearly ten years has passed and helping hundreds of other loyalist researchers has been a large part of my time. In turn, I have acquired a very large library on loyalists and Canada, not to forget the Colonies. My first loyalist lecture was held in 1986 at the Falmouth Genealogical Society in Falmouth (Cape Cod), Massachusetts. There, I discovered that there were many people out there that needed help. My records and sources grew, which gave birth to many written projects, like this one. Hopefully, it will lead the reader to the missing records they seek.

This book was my sixth publication, and now the newly revised edition has been updated to include many more sources, not to forget the Internet. I enjoy this field very much and I have only one to thank; Benjamin Bonnell, UE, my loyalist ancestor. To a Student of research, the truth by telling both sides of history is the most important part of any event. In 1981, I found Benjamin's record in the Provincial Archives at the University of New Brunswick at Fredericton, New Brunswick, Canada. Not knowing the true story of the American Revolution, I thought my ancestor a traitor and turncoat. Then, when I read up on the subject, I found that only one third of the colonies favored separation from Britain. Most people did not want to go against the Throne because it was likened to going against God. Most loyalists were unhappy with all the taxes, but to leave the arms of the mother country was unthinkable. These loyalists were a very brave people who fled to the depths of the Canadian wilderness, a place very hostile at that time in 1783.

The Colonies hold a very special place in world history. It was the birthplace of the first official revolution and the first American Civil War. I wish you all the luck when seeking your loyalist ancestors and when you find one, be proud that you bear the letters U.E. after your name because without them, the United States and Canada would not be as great as they are today.

Even though New Brunswick has celebrated May 18 as "Loyalist Days" for many years, and is privileged with the permission and honor of using a 21 gun salute, Canada has officially designated the first nationally recognized day for the Loyalists on 19 June 1998. Remembering our history and roots is very important to the future generations.

1 *What! I Descend from a Loyalist!*

You are digging deep in old dusty archives trying to find that long-lost ancestor who has been so elusive over many years. You know he lived during the American Revolution and you know what colony (state) he/she lived in, but he/she suddenly disappears when the war breaks out. Hark! Now something turns up—you find a lead! But wait! What kind of lead is this! They are calling him a LOYALIST in the records you find!

What is a LOYALIST?

If you ever wanted an exciting family character to jump out of your closet, a Loyalist will certainly fill the bill with adventure and intrigue. Today, there are millions of Americans who are descendants with this shocking blood running through their once-thought-of-as patriotic veins. Once thought to be a true American, you become ashamed and embarrassed over this find.

"What do I do now?
"Do I hide this person under my rug?

Your next move is to look up who these Loyalists were. Just as you thought! The Loyalists were the people who lost the American Revolution. A Tory! A British Supporter! And Turn-Coat! A Red Coat! A Tar Baby! And all those other labels the Patriots gave them.

"How am I going to tell my All American Yankee father that his ancestor was a traitor! Maybe I should just skip over this guy and tell the family another story!"

This poor genealogist tries to find ways out of his dilemma, but as he reads on about his shocking find, he becomes glued to the pages. The setting is colonial America. The British Empire is trying desperately to keep control of its powerful position in the world as the French and Spanish empires jockey for land all over the New World. The land rush had been going on for over three hundred years, and here progress and history takes its stand in the mid-1700's waiting for the big convulsion to occur.

Wars are being waged on the European continent as well as in the rest of the world. While the French ignore the Acadians in North America, the British move in to take the spoils, but the Acadian farmers are very successful in the cold North, and they must be deported and spread throughout the hemisphere and other lands to break them up. Now, the British Empire can take control of North America in 1755.

The cost of the many wars run high and every British subject must pay their share. Taxes on tea and other items in the colonies will help finance

King George III's conquest of the world. Discontent spreads throughout the land.

Revolt is at hand!

Many of the rich favor secession, and with this small number added to others, separation is popular with only one-third of the colonists, one-third wishing not to take sides and the remaining third never having the thought of going against their King which would be like going against God. They may be struck dead!

We all know what the outcome was, but we hardly ever hear about the losers, the ones that were the establishment. Keep in mind that the Patriots were the rebels, not the British as I was taught in the Los Angeles School system. With great luck on the side of those rebels, the greatest country in the world was born. These losers were not British soldiers, they were American Loyalists who also lived in the colonies, had friends and family members that were Patriots. They were run out and kicked off their lands.

The Treaty of Paris guaranteed the loyalists their right to the lands and property that was taken from them, but the new congress did not ratify that part of the treaty leaving only one choice to the homeless Loyalists.

New York City and area was the British and Loyalists stronghold throughout the war. Refugees from all the colonies and their territories fled to New York City. Washington was obsessed with taking New York, but failed until 1783-84 when hostilities ended. They came from Florida to Massachusetts; they signed up for battle and attacked the entire coastline in return. Conditions were terrible as the refugee's filled barns and warehouses. Life was tough.

At the end of the war one of the greatest exoduses occurred in May 1783. Only one before that was smaller, but with equal impact to the Acadian's when the British expelled them in 1755. Fleet after fleet sailed to Nova Scotia while others fled to London, England, Ontario and Quebec Canada, the Bahamas, and even to Africa.

It became necessary in 1786 to create another Canadian province, New Brunswick. This province was created for the Loyalists, and included the first loyalist city of St. John. This city was founded during the exodus, and later would host riots that were sparked from unfair dealings over supplies and land grants. The last real victim was Benedict Arnold who was burnt in effigy in front of his store in Saint John, leaving his city lot and eight hundred acres in New Brunswick for London where he died a broken man.

These defeated but very brave people cut their way into a hostile wilderness and started life all over again. Replacing the poor Acadians, they were granted land as their payment for their service in the war; even their losses were covered in this manner. The Acadians and Quebec French were by no means out of the picture yet. The ones still living in Canada flourished alongside their new English neighbors, and helped carve out one of the world's greatest countries. How two great countries evolved from a war is beyond reason, but we see it today. Common backgrounds and greatness made these wonderful nations, Canada and the United States of America...

"Hey! These people are not so bad after all," the researcher cries out. He sits up proudly and knows just what he is going to tell his D-Day Invasion and South Pacific Army father--- of course, from a distance at first...

The researcher must keep in mind that these people were run out, they were refugees, fighters and soldiers, and they fled their country. This means, if your Loyalist ancestor was born in one of the colonies, or Britain or Germany, he or she may have been a refugee fleeing to New York City, maybe even dying there or signing up to fight in the Carolinas or Connecticut. He or she may have left New York City in 1783 on one of many fleets that went to areas mentioned in this book.

Possibly your Loyalist ancestor then returned to the United States after the dreadful winter of 1783 in Nova Scotia. Many sneaked back into other states and some even changed their names to return too much warmer climates. Between ten to twenty million Americans today descend from our Canadian brothers to the north. Canada experienced the same westward movement as the U.S. did in the mid-1800, so archives throughout Canada could reveal some family records. Let us not forget the "Prison Ships" that settled Australia and New Zealand. Many of those people were from Canada, and many had Loyalist ancestors. Sierra Leone is another refuge that the "Black Loyalists" went to after bad treatment in Nova Scotia in 1790. Many of these areas have some form of records to help us connect the gaps in our quest for family history.

Today, Loyalist records are scattered in nearly every state and province. The following pages contain areas of importance to the Loyalist-hunter, but keep in mind that there are many others, some small, some big. This work is not made to forget other excellent libraries, archives and societies. This is one main reason why a new edition has been completed; the discovery goes on.

"Remember! It's not an easy find when looking for your Loyalist. It took me ten years!

2 *Canadian Sources*

The National Archives of Canada

395 Wellington Street
Ottawa, Ontario,
Canada K1A 0N3
Phone: 613-995-5138
Reference Service: 613-992-3884
Genealogy Reference: 613-996-7458
Fax# 613-995-6274
Website: http://www.archives.ca/
or ftp://ftp.cac.psu.edu/pub/genealogy/text/guides/can-arch.txt

Once called "The Public Archives of Canada," the National Archives of Canada are your best all-around research location for Loyalists. The staff is excellent and they deal with the public by mail or in person with the highest quality of assistance in mind. There are many records here and the material listed below only pertains to the time period of the Loyalists.

Parish Registers/Census & Other Sources

Cape Breton

Census Showing Possible Loyalists

1811: (Heads of household listed only)

New Brunswick

Sackville, Westmorland County.
Civil Registers
Births and deaths: 1768 – 1822 (microfilm reel # C-3201)

Shediac, Westmorland, County.
St. Martin's Anglican Church
Births, marriages and deaths: 1822 – 1835 (microfilm reel # C-3020)
Includes Bouctouche and Richibouctou.

Sheffield, Sunbury County.
Civil Registers
Births: 1750 – 1829 (microfilm reel # C-3020)
Marriage: 1766 – 1835 (microfilm reel # C-3020)
Deaths: 1766 – 1845 (microfilm reel # C-3020)

Westmorland County.
Civil Registers
Marriages: 1790 – 1835 (microfilm reel # M-828 indexed)

Newfoundland

St. John's.
St. John's Anglican Cathedral
Births, marriages and deaths: 1752 – 1790 (microfilm reel # M-1904)
Includes St. John's district.
Births: 1786 – 1803
Marriages: 1784 – 1795
Deaths: 1795 – 1803

St. John's Congregational Church.
Births: 1780 – 1816 (microfilm reel # M-720)
Marriages: 1802 – 1817, 1834 – 1844 (microfilm reel # M-720)
Deaths: 1837 – 1838 (microfilm reel # M-720)

Trinity.
St. Paul's Anglican Church
Births: 1753 – 1867 (microfilm reel # M-1947)
Marriages and deaths: 1757 – 1867 (microfilm reel # M-1947)

Census for Newfoundland Loyalist
None

Nova Scotia

Annapolis, Annapolis County.
Civil Registers
Births, marriages and deaths: 1747, 1774 – 1874, 1884 (microfilm reel # C-3026 indexed)

Annapolis Methodist Circuit.
Births: 1835 – 1854 (microfilm reel # C-3021)
Marriages: 1834 – 1852 (microfilm reel # C-3021)

St. Luke's Anglican Church.
Births: 1782 – 1817, 1833 – 1888 (microfilm reel # C-3021)
Marriages: 1782 – 1794, 1807 – 1817 (microfilm reel # C-3021)
Deaths: 1808 – 1817 (microfilm reel # C-3021)

St. Luke's Anglican Church, Clements, Granville and Dalhousie.
Marriages: 1806, 1813, 1817 – 1834 (microfilm reel # C-3021)

Aylesford, Annapolis County.
St. Mary's Anglican Church
Births: 1817 – 1861 (microfilm reel # C-3021)

Chester, Lunenburg County.
Civil Registers
Births: 1762 – 1828 (microfilm reel # C-3027)
Marriages: 1775 – 1817 (microfilm reel # C-3927)
Deaths: 1775 – 1818 (microfilm reel # C-3027)

St. Stephen's Anglican Church.
Births: 1762 – 1841 (microfilm reel # C-3021)

Clements, Annapolis County.
St. Edward's Anglican Church
Births: 1841 – 1874 (microfilm reel # C-3021)
Marriages: 1841 – 1911 (microfilm reel # C-3021)

Cornwallis, Digby County.
Cornwallis Baptist Church
Marriages: 1801 – 1822 (microfilm reel # C-3021)

Cornwallis Methodist Church.
Births: 1814 – 1827 (microfilm reel # C-3021)

St. John's Anglican Church.
Births: 1783 – 1902 (microfilm reel # C-3021)
Marriages: 1783 – 1911 (microfilm reel # C-3021)
Deaths: 1830 – 1920 (microfilm reel # C-3021)

Cornwallis Township, Digby County.
Civil Registers
Births, marriages and deaths: 1720 – 1885 (microfilm reel # C-3027)

Cumberland County.
Civil Register
Births, marriages and deaths: 1757 – 1817, 1832 – 1837 (microfilm reel # M-843). Includes the districts of Franklin Manor, Elysian Fields and Nappan.

Digby, Digby County.
Trinity Anglican Church
Births: 1786 – 1830 (microfilm reel # C-2217)
Marriages: 1786 – 1834 (microfilm reel # C-2217)
Deaths: 1786 – 1846 (microfilm reel # C-2217)

Falmouth, Hants County.
Civil Registers
Births, marriages and deaths: 1747 – 1825 (microfilm reel # C-3027)

Fort Lawrence.
Civil Registers
Births, marriages and deaths: 1766 – 1891 (microfilm reel # M-843)
Includes town of Cumberland 1774 – 1813.

Granville, Annapolis County.
Anglican Churches of Granville
Births: 1790 – 1801, 1829 – 1918 (microfilm reel # C-3021)
Marriages: 1790 – 1801, 1814 – 1882 (microfilm reel # 3021 & C-3022)
Deaths: 1828 – 1918 (microfilm reel # C-3022). Includes All Saints Anglican Church, Christ Anglican Church and Trinity Anglican Church.

Granville.
Civil Registers
Births, marriages and deaths: 1720 – 1881 (microfilm reel # C-3027 indexed)

Horton, King's County.
Civil Registers
Births, marriages and deaths: 1823 – 1895 (microfilm reel # C-027 indexed)

St. John's Anglican Church.
Births: 1823 – 1877 (microfilm reel # C-3022)

Liverpool, Queen's County.
Liverpool Methodist Church
Births: 1786 – 1899 (microfilm reel # C-3022)
Marriages: 1816 – 1886 (microfilm reel # C-3022)

Trinity Anglican Church.
Births: 1819 – 1869 (microfilm reel # C-3022)
Marriages: 1820 – 1869 (microfilm reel # C-3022)
Deaths: 1821 – 1869 (microfilm reel # C-3022)

Lunenburg, Lunenburg County.
Lunenburg Baptist Church
Births: 1793 – 1874 (microfilm reel # C-3022)
Marriages: 1819 – 1856 (microfilm reel # C-3022)
Deaths: 1816 – 1858 (microfilm reel # C-3022)

Dutch Reformed Congregation (later, Presbyterian Church).
Births: 1770 – 1926 (microfilm reel # M-2210 & M-2211)
Marriages: 1779 – 1834, 1770 – 1855, 1880 – 1927 (microfilm reel # M-2210 & M-2211)
Deaths: 1771 – 1854, 1880 – 1927 (microfilm reel # M-2210 & M-2211)
Translation (microfilm reel # C-3022)
Communion Rolls: 1780 – 1834 (microfilm reel # M-2210 & M-2211)

Lunenburg Methodist Church.
Births: 1815 – 1837 (microfilm reel # C-3022)
Marriages: 1815 – 1836 (microfilm reel # C-3022)

Newport, Hants County.
Civil Registers
Births: 1752 – 1845 (microfilm reel # C-3027)
Marriages: 1762 – 1856 (microfilm reel # C-3027)
Deaths: 1762 – 1858 (microfilm reel # C-3027)

Onslow, Colchester County.
Civil Register
Births, marriages and deaths: 1761 – 1855, 1896 (microfilm reel # C-3027 indexed)

Rawdon, Hants County.
St. Paul's Anglican Church
Births: 1793, 1809, 1815 – 1880 (microfilm reel # C-3026)
Marriages: 1814 – 1889 (microfilm reel # C-3026)
Deaths: 1815 – 1920 (microfilm reel # C-3026)

Shelburne, Shelburne County.
Christ Church (Anglican)
Births, marriages and deaths: 1783 – 1869 (microfilm reel # C-3026)

Sydney, Cape Breton County.
St. George's Anglican Church
Births: 1785 – 1848 (microfilm reel # C-3026)
Marriages and deaths: 1785 – 1851 (microfilm reel # C-3026)

Truro, Colchester County.
Civil Registers
Births, marriages and deaths: 1761 – 1851 (microfilm reel # C-3026)

Wilmot, Annapolis County.
Trinity Anglican Church
Births, marriages and deaths: 1789 – 1909 (microfilm reel # C-3026)
Includes Aylesford and Bridgetown.

Wilmot Township, Annapolis County.
Civil Registers
Births, marriages and deaths: 1749 – 1894 (microfilm reel # C-1346)

Census in Nova Scotia of Loyalists

1785-1787:	(Heads of household listed only)
1791-1795:	(Heads of household listed only)
1817-1818:	(Heads of household listed only) Incomplete
1827:	(Heads of household listed only) Incomplete
1838:	(Heads of household listed only)
1851:	(Heads of household listed only) Incomplete

Ontario

Cornwall, Stormont County.
Trinity Anglican Church
Births: 1803 – 1846 (microfilm reel # C-3028 indexed)
Marriages: 1803 – 1845 (microfilm reel # C-3028 indexed)
Deaths: 1813 – 1846 (microfilm reel # C-3028 indexed)

Hartford, Norfolk County.
Hartford Baptist Congregation
Births, marriages and deaths: 1783 – 1899 (microfilm reel # M-283)
(Norfolk Historical Society Collection, pp. 12943-12987)

Johnstown District.
Civil Registers
Marriages: 1801 – 1851 (microfilm reel # C-3030 & C-3031) Includes Leeds, Grenville and Carleton Counties.

London District.
Civil Registers
Marriages: 1784 – 1833 (microfilm reel # C-3031 indexed). Includes Norfolk, Oxford and Middlesex Counties.

Sandwich, Essex County.
St. John's Anglican Church
Births, marriages and deaths: 1802 – 1827 (microfilm reel # C-3030 indexed)

Williamsburg, Dunds County.
United Anglican Missions of Williamsburg, Matilda, Osnabruck and Edwardsburg.
Births and marriages: 1790 – 1886 (microfilm reel # M-1496 restricted and indexed)
(Need permission from church to view this film)
Deaths: 1797, 1800 – 1886 (microfilm reel # M-1496 restricted and indexed)
(Need permission from church to view this film)

Williamsburg, Glengarry County.
St. Andrew's Presbyterian Church
Births and marriages: 1779 – 1810 (microfilm reel # C-3030 indexed)
Births, marriages and deaths: 1811 – 1817 (microfilm reel # C-3030 indexed)

Census of possible loyalists
1842: (Heads of household listed only)
1848: (Heads of household listed only) Incomplete
1850: (Heads of household listed only) Incomplete
1851: (All family members listed)

Prince Edward Island

Belfast.
St. John's Presbyterian Church
Births: 1823 – 1849 (microfilm reel # C-3028)

This province has mostly Catholic parishes which consist mainly of the French population. Loyalists who settled here came from New Brunswick and Nova Scotia.

Census Records For Possible Loyalists
1841: (Heads of household listed only)(There is no 1851 census)

Quebec

Clarendon Township, Pontiac County.
Clarendon Anglican Mission
Births, marriages and deaths: 1823 – 1916 (microfilm reel # M-1303 & M-1304 restricted, M-2819 & M-3114). (Permission from church needed to read these reels)

Quebec City.
Quebec Garrison Protestant Church
Births, marriages and deaths: 1787 – 1800, 1817 – 1826 (microfilm reel # C-2898 & C-2899 indexed)

Holy Trinity Anglican Church
Births, marriages and deaths: 1768 – 1800 (microfilm reel # C-2897 & C-2898 indexed)

St. Andrew's Presbyterian Church.
Births, marriages and deaths: 1770 – 1829 (microfilm reel # C-2898)

St. Andrew's East Argenteuil County.
St. Andrew's East Anglican Church
Births, marriages and deaths: 1812 – 1849 (microfilm reel # C-2904 & C-2905)

St. Andrew's East Presbyterian Church.
Births, marriages and deaths: 1818 – 1850 (microfilm reel # C-2905)

Many Catholic Church records go back as far as 1621, but these are not good for Loyalist statistics, only Canadian-French.

Census records for possible loyalists.
1825: (Heads of household listed only)
1831: (Heads of household listed only)
1842: (Heads of household listed only)
1851: (All family members listed)

Manitoba

Loyalists were not granted land here, but the early records will pick up some during the westward movement.

Census Records
1832, 1834, 1835, 1840, 1843, 1846, 1849

Sasktchewan

N/A

Alberta

N/A

British Columbia

N/A

Anglican Church Records Location

Anglican Church of Canada
General Synod Archives
Church House
600 Jarvis Street
Toronto, Ontario, Canada M4Y 2S6

Baptist Church Records Location

Baptist Federation of Canada
Box 1298, Brantford, Ontario
Canada N3T 5T6

Presbyterian Church Records Location

Presbyterian Church of Canada
59 St. George St.
Toronto, Ontario, Canada M5S 2E6

Other Loyalist Sources Located at the National Archives

Ontario was the only province to have a Loyalist list drawn up. In 1796 this list was put into the Crown Lands Office and the Executive Council. Between these there were some discrepancies. The Crown Lands list appears on microfilm reel # C-2222 (this is a transcript). A copy of the original list is on microfilm reel # C-1476.

Loyalist claims for losses can be found on microfilm reel # C-9821. These claims are copies of the lists that are housed in the Public Record Office in London, England.

The Sir Frederick Haldimand Papers, which are housed in the British Library, are at this location on microfilm reel # C-1475. This list contains Muster Rolls and Provincial lists. Some names of dependents are mentioned. Other Muster Rolls are located in the Ward Chipman Papers. This is also on microfilm, but not indexed.

The first Canadian census was in 1851, and this first year will show some old surviving Loyalists and their widows. Very little is listed in the 1861 census. There were, however, many earlier censuses which could be of help.

Books on the Archives

List of Parish Registers Held at the Public Archives of Canada. Revised 1 August 1985. Compiled by John E. Coderre and Paul A. Lavoie. This book can be ordered by the Ottawa Branch of the Ontario Genealogical Society, Ottawa, Ontario, Canada.

Births, Marriages and Death Records

There are not many vital records that go back to the Loyalist period for the provinces. Most start mid-1800s to late 1800s.

Note: A few marriage records are available for Lower Canada (Quebec): 1779 and 1818 – 1867; and Upper Canada (Ontario): 1803 – 1845. Both are indexed and are on microfilm.

Cemetery Records

Much of Ontario has been recorded and the archives have many other areas, but you must know the town or township and the person's religious denomination to locate them.

Indian Records/Native People

In the past they were not regarded as participants in the Revolutionary War. But records find that they played a large part, serving in the war and granted land after. There is much written about Chief Joseph Brant who was a Loyalist.

Land Records

The archives have many land grants, mostly land petitions for Quebec and Lower Canada for 1764 – 1841, and for Upper Canada for 1791 – 1867. These are all indexed and are on microfilm. Each province has its own records on land grants, including some original copies.

Deeds and Other Land Records

Each provincial archive is responsible for housing these records.

Estate Records

These are also in the hands of each provincial archive. Do not forget to check closely in this area because it is a very valuable source for family information.

Military and Naval Records

Most records were not kept until this century, but some very early files were and still are housed at the Public Records Office, London, England. Loyalist records can be found in "Record Group 8, Series 1," giving Muster Rolls and Units, and Muster Rolls for the War of 1812 as well. Record # RG 19 has request for losses claims as a result of American and British attacks in Upper Canada, 1812 – 1814. These are arranged by district and can be found on microfilm # C-15720.

The archives has a specialized list which contains the following:

The British Army Lists, printed from 1754
The British Sea Officers, 1717 – 1815
The Navy List, 1814. (Served similarly for the Royal Navy).

The following list of regiments can be found at the archives which were formed in much of the colonies.

Armed Batteau-men
Armed Bostmen
Arnold's American Legion
Black Pioneers
British Legion
Buck's County Light Dragoons

Collbeck's Company
Carolina King's Rangers
DeDiemar's Hussars
DeLancey Brigade
Emmerick's Chasseurs Dragoons
Ferguson's Corps
Georgia Light Dragoons
New Jersey Volunteers
New York Volunteers
North Carolina Dragoons
North Carolina Highlanders
North Carolina Volunteers
Pennsylvania Loyalists
Philadelphia Light Dragoons
Prince of Wales American Regiment
Provincial Light Infantry
Queen's Rangers
Roger's King's Rangers (Roman Catholic Volunteers)
Georgia Loyalists
Governor Wentworth's Volunteers
Independent Troops of Cavalry
King's American Dragoons
King's American Regiment
King's Orange Rangers
Loyal American Rangers
Loyal American Regiment
Loyal Foresters
Loyal New Englanders
Loyal Nova Scotia Volunteers
Maryland Loyalists
Nassau Blues
Royal American Reformers
Royal Fencible Americans
Royal Garrison Battalion
Royal Guides and Pioneers
Royal North Carolina Regiment
South Carolina Dragoons
South Carolina Rangers
South Carolina Royalist
Volunteers of Ireland
Volunteers of New England
West Florida Foresters
West Jersey Volunteers
Young Royal Highland Emigrants

Also, the following is found in the Northern Canadian Division records:

The King's Royal Regiment of New York, commanded by Sir John Johnson, 1776-1777.

Butler's Rangers, commanded by Lt. Col. John Butler, 1776-1777

Queen's Loyal Rangers, commanded by Lt. Col. John Peters. Raised in 1777.

Royal Americans, commanded by Lt. Col. Ebenezer Jessup. Started in 1777.

Roger's King's Rangers. Raised in 1781-2. Major McAlpine's Royal Americans.

Major Holland's Loyal Yorkers.

MacKay's Loyal Volunteers.

Capt. Robert Leake's Independent Company.

The First Battalion of the 84th, or Royal Highland Regiment, raised by Col. Allen MacLean in 1775.

The following British Military and Naval Records are located at the archives in the Manuscript Record Group # 8 (Loyalist Regiment Muster Rolls, 1777-1783. Volumes 1851 – 1908, 7 feet, 8 inches).

Volumes		Number of Pages
1851-1860	New Jersey Volunteers, 1777-83	1009
1861-1866	Queen's Rangers, 1777-82	416
1867-70	Loyal American Regiment, 1777-83	375
1871-72	American Legion, 1781-82	122
1873	Royal Garrison Battalion, 1778-83	41
1874-75	New York Volunteers, 1777-83	107
1867-82	DeLancey's Brigade, 1777-83	1158
1883-85	British Legion, 1778-83	253
1886-87	Volunteers of Ireland, 1778-82	115
1888-89	Guides and Pioneers, 1779-83	168
1890	South Carolina Royalists, 1779-82	24
1891	Emerick's Chasseurs, 1781	38
1892	Loyal New Englanders, 1778	33
1892	Loyal Foresters, 1781-82	33
1892	King's Rangers, 1783	33
1893	Royal Fencible American Regiment, 1777	28
1893	Volunteers of New England, 1782	28
1894	Royal American Reformers, 1778	35
1894-97	Prince of Wales American Regiment, 1777-79	206
1898	Carolina King's Rangers, 1777-82	27
1899	South Carolina Rangers, 1780-88	15
1899	South Carolina Dragons, 1781	15
1900	Provincial Light Infantry, 1781	35
1900	Roman Catholic Volunteers, 1777-78	35
1901	The King's American Dragoons, 1782-83	89
1902	South Carolina Royalist, 1781-83	72
1902-03	The King's American Regiment, 1779-83	105
1904-05	Maryland Loyalists, 1777-83	127
1906-07	Pennsylvania Loyalists, 1777-83	107
1907	United Pennsylvania and Maryland Loyalists, 1780	59
1908	The King's Orange Rangers, 1777-78	Unknown

RECORDS FOUND IN OTHER LOCATIONS OF CANADA

NEWFOUNDLAND & LABRADOR

The Provincial Archives of Newfoundland & Labrador

Colonial Building, Military Road
St. John's, Newfoundland, Canada A1C 2C9
Phone: 709-753-9390

Births, Marriages & Deaths

There are some records that date as far back as 1820, but it is not known if they contain any Loyalists.

Note: Parish records are located at the National Archives of Canada and are listed in this book.

Societies

Newfoundland Historical Society
Colonial Bldg., Military Rd., Rm. 15
St. John's, Newfoundland,
Canada A1C 2C9
Phone: 709-722-3191
Note: They are on the Internet.

Newfoundland & Labradore Genealogical Society
Colonial Building, Military Rd.
St. John's Newfoundland,
Canada A1C 2C9
Phone: 709-754-9525
E-mail Address: nlgs@nf.sympatico.ca
Website: http://www3.nf.sympatico.ca/nlgs/
Office Location: 354 Water St., Room 421, St. John's, NF

Newfoundland & Labradore Internet Locations

Newfoundland & Labradore GenWeb Page
Website: http://www.huronweb.com/genweb/nf.htm

The Newfoundland & Labradore Genealogy Page
Website: http://www.iosphere.net/~jholwell/cangene/nl.html

Newfoundland & Labradore Genealogy Research Interests Forum
Website: http://www3.ns.sympatico.ca/crant/nlgrif-l.html

NOVA SCOTIA

Nova Scotia Archives & Records Management

6016 University Ave.
Halifax, Nova Scotia, Canada B3H 1W4
Phone: 902-424-6060
Fax: 902-424-0628
E-mail: nsarm@gov.ns.ca

Census (Pertaining to Loyalists)

1770-1771:	(Heads of Household) before Loyalist period.
1785-1787:	(Heads of Household)
1781-1795:	(Heads of Household)
1817-1818:	(Heads of Household) Incomplete
1827:	(Heads of Household) Incomplete
1838:	(Heads of Household) Incomplete
1851:	(Heads of Household) Incomplete

Marriages

They have some dating as far back as the late 1700s.

Land Grants

Original land grants are held not at the archives, but at the Crown Lands Office, Department of Lands and Forests, Halifax, Nova Scotia, Canada B3J 2T9. The archives has copies and they are filed with petitions for grants which are indexed.

Estate Records

Copies of Probate records dated before 1900 are located here at the archives. Some are indexed, but all records are at the Registry of Probate in each county.

General Loyalist Information

Over 100 books and printed materials on Loyalists covering all aspects of the Loyalists' lives and adventures, including many lists of Loyalists, battles fought, ships sailed, and genealogies. Research service is not available over the e-mail system at this archives.

Black Loyalists of Nova Scotia

Many blacks were freed during the American Revolution by the British as long as they served the King in the conflict. They were given land grants in Nova Scotia and New Brunswick, but were still treated differently because they received 50 acres where the whites of the same rank received 100 to 200 acres. By 1790, discord and riots broke out and leaders of the black community went to England to seek ships to take them to Sierra Leone, Africa. This occurred, but met disaster when they arrived with very little to start life again. Over half the population was wiped out.

The archives contains over 30 books and printed materials on these brave people which numbered around 3,000.

Example: *The Blacks in Canada, A History.* By Robin W. Winks (hardcover), Pub. by McGill-Queen's University Press, Montreal, Canada & Yale University Press, New Haven, Conn. 1971.

Loyalist Political Materials & Books

There are several biographical sketches on the leaders or outstanding Loyalists of the time which is an excellent source.

The Affairs of Business of the Loyalists

Over 20 books and articles on shipping, trade and economic matters which include the steamship industry, the early post office, and merchant letters and diaries.

Other Loyalists Societies

This archives contains a few titles about different organizations that Loyalists either started or were involved in, such as:

The Saint Andrews Lodge
The Grand Lodge
Freemasons
The Halifax Poor Man's Friend Society
The North British Society
The Society for the Relief of the Poor

Religions of the Loyalists

Listing over 50 sources of materials on this subject, but the researcher must keep in mind that most Loyalists were members of the Church of England, Anglicans, but there were many Quakers who were caught up in this struggle and they too had to leave the colonies for the northern provinces. There were other religious groups, including Methodists, Baptists (later), and Presbyterians.

Most of this material is biographical in nature, but some contains lists of members and histories of those parishes.

Note: Parish records for the province are located at the Canadian National Archives, and some may need permission for access.

Education of the Loyalists

Over 20 books and articles dealing with educational matters such as funding, conditions, provisions, policies and the historical background of the King's College in Halifax which began approx. 1750.

Loyalist Literature

Over 20 works dealing with Loyalist literature, including poetry, memoirs and notes, many written by the clergy.

Newspapers

Over 25 books or materials dealing with the early Loyalist newspapers, including some taken from Acadian sources listing prominent people in the field such as John Howe and Jotham Blanchard. Some outstanding newspapers were:

The Acadian and General Advertiser, 1827-1829
Acadian Recorder, 1813-1930
Colonial Patriot, 1827-1834
Free Press, 1816-1834
Halifax Journal, 1781-1810, 1810-1854
Nova Scotia Gazette and Weekly Chronicle, 1770-1789
Nova Scotia Packet and General Advertiser, 1785-1796
Novascotian or Colonial Herald, 1824-1840
Novator and Nova Scotia Literary Gazette, 1808-1810
Port Roseway Gazette and Shelburne Advertiser, 1784-1785
Royal American Gazette, 1783-1785
Royal Gazette and Nova Scotia Advertiser, 1789-1800
Weekly Chronicle, 1786-1826

Loyalist Architecture

Over a score of books and articles on the building styles of the Loyalists, including government houses, private homes and churches, many of which emulate New England styles.

Miscellaneous Materials on Loyalists at the Archives

Various written material on nearly all the Loyalist communities in Nova Scotia, including military records, hardships encountered, some obituaries, settlements, grants, daily life, diaries and genealogies. Much is written on Shelburne.

Genealogies of Loyalists

This section is being added to all the time. The following is a list of just a few of the main characters mentioned: Mary Berry, the Boggs Family, John Brown, Elizabeth Deering, James Delancey, the Dukeshire Family, the Edison Family (that is Thomas Edison line), Andrew Forshner, Abraham Gesner, Henry Gesner, Joseph Giles, George Gillmore, Garret Grovestine, the Halliburton Family, Irad Hart, Josiah Hart, John Hatfield, Adam Hemeon, John Higgins, John & Joseph Howe, Charles Inglis, John Inglis,

Hezekiah Ingraham, John Smith Lowe, the Mair Family, Garrett & Joseph Miller, Thomas Millidge, Daniel, James & Jonathan Morehouse, Donald & Hugh McKay, Andrew McKim, Nicholas Purdue, Alex Peers, John Sargent, Daniel Soules, the Stevens Family, the Sulis Family, Alexander John Thomson, Georg Josef Tuchsherer, Stephen Tuttle, William Wells.

Loyalist Military Records

Over 25 books and articles on Loyalists who served in the military during the American Revolution, including rolls, lists of black soldiers, biographical sketches of famous men such as David Fanning, James Moody, the DeLancey brothers, Benedict Arnold, Howe, etc.

Loyalist Bibliographies

Lists about 15 bibliographies, but contains some births, deaths, and marriages, and some American sources located at the Library of Congress and National Archives in Washington D.C. Also, Wills, Nova Scotia Vital Statistics, and some various histories.

Books & Materials on Loyalists

The Loyalist Guide, Nova Scotia Loyalists and Their Documents. Compiled by Jean Peterson. Pub. by The Public Archives of Nova Scotia, 1983. (This book is one of the best for Loyalist material that is located at the archives. I recommend you read this before going there to do your research. It breaks down nearly every Loyalist record available, even the location numbers.) Available at the archives.

This Unfriendly Soil, The Loyalist Experience in Nova Scotia 1783-1791, by Neil MacKinnon. Pub. by McGill-Queen's University Press. (date unknown). Available at the archives.

King's Bounty. A history of early Shelburne, by Marion Robertson, Pub. by Nova Scotia Museum, Halifax, NS, 1983. From 1783 to 1800's. History of the Loyalists. Available at the archives.

Loyalists in Nova Scotia. Edited by Donald Wetmore & Lester B. Sellick, Pub. by Lancelot Press, Hantsport, NS, 1983. About the people and how they lived as Loyalists and settlers. Available at the archives.

Loyalist Foods in Today's Recipes. By Eleanor Robertson Smith, Pub. by Lancelot Press, Hantsport, NS, 3rd printing, August 1984.

Loyalists and Land Settlement in Nova Scotia.
By Marion Gilroy, 1937, Nova Scotia.

Nova Scotia Newspapers.
By NS Hist. & Gene. Societies, started 1981.
Covers 1765 & up.

Planters & Pioneers.
By Dr. Esther Clark Wright. Revised edition, 1982. Printed by Lancelot Press, NS.

Genealogical Research in Nova Scotia.
By Terrence M. Punch. Pub. by NS Archives, 1983.

Nova Scotia Published Diaries

No Place Like Home
By Conrad, Laid and Smyth, 1988.
Diaries and letters of Nova Scotia Women 1771-1938.

Benjamin Marston's Diary.
Published Collections #8 of New Brunswick Historical Society.
Information about Shelburne.

Loyalist Period Sites to See When Traveling

The Prince of Wales Martello Tower

Fort Edward

Port Royal

Fort Anne

Loyalist Burying Ground
Downtown Halifax, NS
Historical site & resting place for many Loyalists.

Societies

Royal Nova Scotia Historical Society
c/o Dr. Allan Marble (as of 1990)
6366 South St.
Halifax, NS B3H 1T9

Shelburne Historical Society
c/o Francis Atkinson (as of 1990)
Box 39
Shelburne, NS B0T 1W0

The Genealogical Association of Nova Scotia
P.O. Box 641 Station "Central"
Halifax, NS B3J 2T3
Phone: 902-454-0322
E-mail: ip-gans@chebucto.ns.ca
Website: http://www.ccn.cs.dal.ca/Recreation/GANS/gans_homepage.html
(They produce The Nova Scotia Genealogist Magazine)

South Shore Genealogical Society
68 Bluenose Dr. P.O. Box 901
Lunenburg, Nova Scotia B0J 2C0
Phone: 902-634-4794
E-mail: ssgsoc@hotmail.com

Shelburne County Genealogical Society
168 Water St. P.O. Box 248
Shelburne, NS B0T 1W0
Phone: 902-875-4299
E-mail: loyaler@mail.bar.auracom.com

Nova Scotia Internet Locations

Nova Scotia GenWeb Page
Website: http://www.geocities.com/Heartland/6625/nsgenweb.html

Nova Scotia Genealogy
Website: http://www.ced.tuns.ca/~parkerb/

Beaton Institute Archives
Website: http://www.eagle.uccb.ns.ca/beaton/beaton.html

Beaton Genealogy Database
http://eagle.uccb.ns.ca/beaton2/menus/biomenu.html

Nova Scotia Regional Libraries
Website: http://rs6000.nshpl.library.ns.ca:80/regionals/

Lunenburg County GenWeb Page
Website: http://www.geocities.com/Heartland/6625/index.html

Pictou County, Family Roots
Website: http://www.rootsweb.com/~pictou
Has Loyalist ship passenger lists, Speedwell, Ann and Hector. Also other records.

Pictou County Nova Scotia GenWeb Page
Website: http://www.rootsweb.com/~nspictou

CAPE BRETON

(Separated From Nova Scotia)
(Records at Nova Scotia Archives)

Cape Breton was part of Nova Scotia until 1784 when it separated from Halifax as New Brunswick did, but Cape Breton was reunited with Nova Scotia in 1820. Nearly 30 books and written material on this short lived province, including:

Census of 1811 & 1818

Marriage records of 1799 to 1809

Cape Breton Internet Locations

Cape Breton GenWeb Page
Website: http://www.geocities.com/Heartland/Plains/1368/cbgenwb.html
Lists family genealogies and other sources.

PRINCE EDWARD ISLAND

The Public Archives of Prince Edward Island

P.O. Box 1000
Charlottetown, Prince Edward Island, Canada C1A 7M4
Phone: 902-368-4290

Census (pertaining to Loyalists)

1841 (Heads of household)

Marriage & Baptismal Records

If there are Loyalist marriage records here, it would be a small collection dating before 1886.

Land Records

The archives holds all land records on microfilm before 1900.

Estate Records

Probate court records dating 1815-1933 are located here.

Church Records

Parish records found at the Canadian National Archives are listed in this book.

Loyalist Period Sites to See When Traveling

Province House
Fort Amherst/Port LaJoye

Societies

Prince Edward Island Genealogical Society
Box 902, 2 Kent St.
Charlottetown, P.E.I., C1A 7M4

United Empire Loyalists' Association, Abegweit Branch
c/o Mary Bradshaw (as of 1998)
326 Maple Ave.
Summerside, PEI
Canada C1N 2H3

P.E.I Internet Connections

United Empire Loyalists' Association, Abeqweit Branch, PEI
Page Location: http://www.isn.net/~dhunter/uel.html
This site provides information about the PEI branch and lists muster rolls and loyalist lineages, etc.

PEI Gen Web Provincial Page.
Page Location: http://www.isn.net/~dhunter/pegenweb.html

PEI Arrivals/Departures Database.
Page Location: http://www.isn.net/~dhunter/ship_data.html

PEI Genealogical Society Home Page.
Page Location: http://www.isn.net/~dhunter/peigs.html

The Island Register Online Bookstore.
http://www.isn.net/~dhunter/bookstore.html

PEI Surname Register
Website: http://www.geocities.com/Heartland/Acres/4835/index.html
A listing and contact site.

PEI Listing of Genealogy Sites
Website: http://www.peisland.com/fyi/genealog/genealog.html

Provincial Library Service
Website: http://www.gov.pe.ca/educ/library/index.asp

Repositories in Charlottetown, PEI
Website: http://www.gov.pe.ca/educ/archives/fam_history/repo_char.asp

Books & Materials of P.E.I. Loyalists

An Island Refuge
Compiled by Abegweit Branch, UEL, 1983

NEW BRUNSWICK

The Provincial Archives of New Brunswick

P.O. Box 6000
The University of New Brunswick, Canada
Fredericton, New Brunswick, Canada E3B 5H1
Phone: 505-453-2637 or 505-453-2122

Census (pertaining to Loyalist Period)

1783 – Heads of household. This is a passenger list from New York to Saint John. This list indicates if there was a wife and children, the ship name and sometimes which colony they came from and occupation. This source is found in the book: *Early Loyalist Saint John,* by D.G. Bell, Pub. by New Ireland Press, 1983 (Not a complete list).

1784 – Heads of household. This is a list of who survived the winter after the 1783 exodus from New York. (Not a complete list - found in *Early Loyalist Saint John,* by D.G. Bell – see above).

1851 – Lists all members of family. This census will show the surviving Loyalists by the date they came to Canada (1783). Some will also state that they are Loyalists).

Vital Statistics from Newspapers

A very large collection, nearly complete. Also contains the many volumes of Vital Statistics from New Brunswick Newspapers, by Daniel F. Johnson, self published, going from 1783 to nearly 1900.

Family History Index

A large collection of family histories, many donated by private parties in book form, microfilmed, documents in files.

County Records

This collection is in files/binders, and contains church, marriage and epitaph records, listed by county.

Index Cards

Listed for family, local and church history. (Microfilm Subject Card Index).

Epitaph listings taken from various sources. (Vital Statistic Card Index).

Biographical sketches in different forms (Biographical Card Index).

Various publications (New Brunswick Publications MC80 Index).

Land Petitions

1784-1850 Card Index (RG10, RS108). Some contain biographical information.

1830 – Present, Card Index, current series (RS272). There is little data here.

Court Records

Supreme Court Records (RG5, RS189) Card file, 1795-1901.

Intermediate Court Records (RG6) Card file. Most counties represented.

Supreme Court Records: Original Jurisdiction (RG5, RS42) Card file, 1784-1822.

Court of Equity: Original Jurisdiction (RG5, RS55) Card file, 1784-1910 (10,000 files).

Marriage Bonds & Licenses

Card file for years 1810 to 1900 (RG3, RS551). Not complete.

Manuscript Records

This is a very large collection of early family, historical, newspaper and directory information (Over 1400 collections).

Probate Records

The original copies of wills, inventories, or other probate records are now stored off-site because of space problems. The copies are all on microfilm.

Government Records

Administration of Estate records of Deceased Insolvent Debtors (RS575), 1784-1843.

Provincial Secretary Records of Old Soldiers and Widows (RS566), 1839-1868 (Over 400 files).

Department of Justice records, Land Registry Office from 1784 to c. 1970. Has deeds, mortgages and leases on most counties.

Department of Education, Licensing and Appointment records (RS115), 1816-1967. Teacher Petitions and License (RS655), 1812-1882, Indexed, 23 microfilm reels. Grammar, Private schools and Parish returns (RS657), 1816-1971

Department of Health Records

Birth records (RS141), 1810-1887, 25,000 index cards.

Land Grant Records

Survey maps and land grants dated 1785-1986. Indexed and on microfiche.

Maps of land grants showing Loyalists can be purchased at The Lands Branch, Dept. of Natural Resources, P.O. Box 6000, Fredericton, NB E3B 5H1.

Books & Materials

One book that is a must to get is by Robert Fellows, *Researching Your Ancestors in New Brunswick*, Pub. by the Archives, 1979. This is the best source of the Archives listings until a new revised version comes along.

Hundreds of other books on Loyalists, most that are mentioned in this book are carried at the archives.

The archives updates a very large selection of holdings listed by county. This is available upon request.

Loyalist Period Sites & Historical Locations in New Brunswick

Kings Landing Historical Settlement

Exit 259 off Rt. 2
35 km. West of Fredericton
P.O. Box 522
Kingsclear, New Brunswick, Canada E3B 5A6
Phone: 506-363-5805

This is a Loyalist settlement open to the public from June to October, but has special events around Christmas. This is a very large historical village recreated by experts in Loyalist studies. When visiting, be prepared to do a lot of walking as each road takes you back in time while seeing many Loyalist homes, farms and Inns. Listed below are some structures:

Hagemann House, 1870
Joslin Farm, 1860
A Sawmill, 1730
A Gristmill, 1880
Lint House, 1830
Blacksmith Shop, 1870
St. Mark's Church, 1890
Perley House, 1870
Grant Store, 1890
Morehouse House, 1820
School, 1840
Print Shop, 1890
Kings Head, Inn

The village is being added to all the time. There is a fine gift shop, The Emporium carries many items on New Brunswick, and the Loyalists.

Books on Kings Landings

Kings Landing Country, Life in Early Canada, by Wayne Barrett with introduction by Dr. George MacBeath, Pub. by Oxford University Press, Toronto, Canada, 1979 & reprinted by Nimbus, Halifax, N.S., 1989. Photos of village by Wayne Barrett.

Today, I believe there is a video on the Kings Landing Settlement.

The Harding House
(Formerly, The Benjamin Bonnell, UE, Homestead, c. 1786)

Hardings Point Campground
Westfield, New Brunswick, Canada E0G 3J0
Phone: 506-763-2517
Owners & Proprietors: Diane & Howard Heans

The property is located where the Westfield Ferry lands at Long Reach about 12 miles north of Saint John City. Approx. a 400 acres campground site, the Harding House now serves as a store, but is being restored by the Heans family. Benjamin Bonnell built the first section of the house around 1786 (My previous edition placed the date at 1790, but this has been corrected to 1786) when he received a 200 acre land grant from King George III for his service in the Revolutionary War. After 1811, the house changed hands a few times and ended up in the Harding family where they expanded it to its present look.

It became a famous rest stop and Inn during the riverboat era (c. 1850-c. 1910). Many passengers rested there on their way between Fredericton and Saint John. The home is rich in Canadian Loyalist history and loyalist artifacts have been discovered all around the home, including a c. 1780's loyalist boys jacket with a fishing pole in between the ancient walls of the old Bonnell section found in May 1988. Today, the campground is a fine place to visit and the view of the Saint John River couldn't be any better. Howard and Diane Heans are still working hard at rebuilding the home to its original grandeur.

Other Loyalist Sites & Locations

Carleton Martello Tower
St. Andrew's Blockhouse
St. Andrew's, New Brunswick

Loyalist Burying Ground

Downtown Center, Saint John City
New Brunswick

The first burial place for Loyalists was set aside in 1783, and the first burial was in 1784. Many Loyalist families had to wait several months or years for a gravestone for their loved ones because the only place the stones came from was the New England States (mainly New Hampshire) and from Scotland and England. No real Loyalist would have a Yankee stone on his final resting place. The New Brunswick Historical Society and The Saint John Branch of The United Empire Loyalists' Association have taken an active part in keeping this historical landmark presentable for all to enjoy.

Market Square

Saint John Wharf
Saint John City, New Brunswick

The original landing spot of the Loyalists in 1783 is now a mall and market area. Near the waters edge is a plaque commemorating the Loyalist landing and during Loyalist Days in May each year, flowers and activities take place around the historical location. An old school house converted into a general store is located just a few feet away for the tourists to explore old wares.

City of St. Andrews

Located in the southwestern corner of New Brunswick, this small community was founded by the Loyalists. A visit there is worth it because many of the fine old New England construction still stands. All the bright white buildings makes this a picture-perfect scene along the Bay of Fundy. Their neighbor is Castine, Maine.

Other New Brunswick Research Sites & Societies

The following institutions can be contacted and contain Loyalist material.

The United Empire Loyalists' Association of Canada, Saint John Branch. P.O. Box 6044 Station A, Saint John, New Brunswick, Canada E2L 4R5

The United Empire Loyalists' Association of Canada, Fredericton Branch (Most recent address is not available. Check with National Headquarters for recent director in charge)

The New Brunswick Genealogical Society, P.O. Box 3235 Station B, Fredericton, New Brunswick, Canada E3A 5G9 (There are many branches located throughout New Brunswick)

Mount Allison University
Archives Section
Sackville, New Brunswick,
Canada

They have a large Loyalist collection.

The New Brunswick Museum, Archives, Library Section

277 Douglas Ave.,
Saint John, New Brunswick,
Canada E2K 1E5
Phone: 506-658-1842.

Many records were given to the Saint John Regional Library, but some of the following records and materials can be found at their location above or the annex site at the Market Square Mall (Please inquire).

Abaco, Bahama Islands: *Notes on the Loyalist settlements in Hope Town, Abaco, Bahamas*, by Rev. E. H. Sumner

Adair, Robert: Agreement of sale between himself and David McClure, both of York county, 1786.

Allen, Col. Isaac: Appointment as colonel to York County regiment, 1787.

Anderson, William: Appointment to clerk of Assembly, 1807, Saint John.

Annapolis Royal, Nova Scotia: Account book of merchants, possibly Mr. Walker, 1791-96.

Arnold, Benedict: Legel papers and correspondence, 1783-1802.

Bailey, Phillip: Memo of Peter Clinch, real estate of his in Charlotte County, c. 1786.

Beck, Mary: of Saint John, letter from her aunt, Mary Stokes of Philadelphia, 1792.

Belding, Daniel: Account book of his, seaman and merchant, settled at Chance Harbour, 1797-1841.

Berton, Peter: Agreement to purchase land from Col. Stephen Kemble, 1786. Deed for church and burial ground at Oak Point, 1788.

Bliss, Jonathan: Legal papers, 1790-1819.

Blowers, Sampson Salter: Business papers, 1781-1822.

Boggs, John: Deeds to Philip Schurman and James Clark of Saint John, 1795, 1796.

Botsford Family: Papers of Amos Botsford of Westmorland County, 1784-1839.

Brill Family: Deeds, commissions and will of Jacob Brill of Queen's County, 1801-44.

Calef, Dr. John: Letter to John Perkins, Joseph Perkins and Mark Hatch, 1789.

Camp Family: Letters, 1803-16.

Canby, Joseph: Certificates for lot in Saint John, 1784.

Carleton, Lt. Gov. Thomas: Correspondence, 1784-86.

Chaloner Family: Certificates for lots, 1784.

Charlotte County: Deeds, accounts, bonds, leases and petitions, 1784-67.

Chipman, Ward: Letters and legal papers, 1764-1879.

Chubb Family: Two letters, 1789, 1801.

Clark Family: Land deeds, New Jersey and New Brunswick, 1727-83. Also contains an arithmetic work book, 1763.

Clark, Dugald: Discharge from 74th Regiment, 1783.

Clarke, Richard: Appointment as missionary in New Brunswick, 1799.

Clopper, Garret: Letter-book, 1803-6. Also contains notebook of accounts, 1790-95.

Coffin Family: Affidavit of John Coffin, Major in the Kings American Regiment, 1797 and grant to son Henry, 1821.

Company for the Propagation of the Gospel: Mentions George Leonard, Ward Chipman, John Coffin, Edward Winslow, Joshua Upham, William Hazen, George Sproule and William Hazen Jr., 1808.

Crookshank Family: Legal papers, 1786-1887 and other family documents.

Other documents containing various family information are: Davison, DePeyster, Dibblee, Drake, Earle, Easton, Fanning, Flewelling, Fowler, Gallant, Ganong, Gaunce, Gilbert, Gordon, Gunter, Hamilton, Harding, Hardy, Hendricks, Higgenbotham, Hubbard, Huestis, Jarvis, Jordan, Keaquick, Kent, Knight, Lane, Lee, Leonard, Lingley, Lorrain, MacKenzie, McLean, McNeal, Mayes, Melick, Menzies, Merritt, Moore, Morris, Mowat, Muir, Mullin, Munro, Murray, Myline, Nase, Odell, Otty, Pagan, Paine, Pickett, Powell, Puddington, Regan, Reid, Robinson, Sears, Sewell, Shaw, Sickles, Smith, Somers, Speed, Spragg, Stackhouse, Supplee, Thomson, Taylor, Thorn, Tilton, Vanderbrugh, Van Wart, Waltman, Ward, Webster, Wetmore, Whitney, Willard, Winslow, Wyer, Yeamans.

Other Loyalist records administered by the museum are:

Passamaquoddy muster rolls, 1784.
Black Pioneers muster rolls, 1779-80.
British Legion muster rolls, 1782.
DeLancey's Brigade, 3rd Battalion, 1781 & 1783.
Guides and Pioneers muster roll, 1779-80.
King's American Dragoons, 1782.
King's American Regiment muster rolls, 1777-78.
King's New Brunswick Regiment, 1793-97.
Loyal American Regiment muster rolls, 1777-78.
New Jersey Volunteers, 1778.
New Jersey Volunteers, 2nd Battalion muster roll, 1781.
New York Volunteers muster roll, 1777.
Prince of Wales Royal American Volunteers muster roll, 1777-78.
Queen's Rangers muster roll, 1780.
Wentworth's Volunteers, 1778.
Kings County, New Brunswick account book, possibly Sussex area, 1791-1800.
Kings County land grant, Studholme, Hayes, Harper, Burgess, MacLeod, 1784.
New Brunswick Chancery Court records, 1785-1823.
New Brunswick Legislative Council records, 1786-1802.
New Brunswick Secretary's Office Memo book, 1784-1809.
New Brunswick Supreme Court records, 1785-1809.
Saint John, Exchange CoffeeHouse list, 1803-4.
Saint John, Merchant's daybook, 1787-88 & 1793-95, 1798 & 1801-2.

Saint John City, register of voters, 1785-1860.
Saint John County Poll book, 1802.
Sussex Indian Academy documents, 1787-1832.
Westmorland County marriage bonds, 1786-1811.

Diaries:

Col. Henry Nase (Loyalist)

The following book is a good source for the museum's holdings:

The New Brunswick Museum Department of Canadian History Archives Division. Inventory of Manuscripts (1967). Published privately by the museum.

Books & Materials For New Brunswick Research

In Search of Your Roots. By Angus Baxter. A guide for Canadian research. Pub. by Macmillan of Canada. Revised and reprinted 1984.

Researching Your Ancestors in New Brunswick, Canada, by Robert F. Fellows, Pub. 1979 by The New Brunswick Archives.

Thunder Over New England, Benjamin Bonnell, *The Loyalist.* By Paul J. Bunnell, FACG, UE. Pub. by Christopher Pub., 1988. Life of a loyalist family.

The New Loyalist Index, Vols. I, II, III. By Paul J. Bunnell, FACG, UE. Pub. by Heritage Books, Inc., Bowie, MD.

Loyalists All. By Gail Bonsall Pipes. Pub. by UEL, New Brunswick Branch, 1985. Lists of loyalists and their families and descendants.

Early Marriages of New Brunswick. By B. Wood-Holt. Pub. by Holland House, 1986.

Vital Statistics From New Brunswick Newspapers. By Daniel F. Johnson, B.B.A.,C.G. ©. Saint John, New Brunswick. Pub. by Vital Statistics Committee & Johnson. Volumes dated from 1786 to approx. 1900.

New Brunswick Loyalists. By Sharon Debeau. Pub. by Generation Press, Agincourt, Ontario, 1983. Biographies of Loyalists.

Early Loyalist Saint John, 1783-1786. By D.G. Bell. Pub. by New Ireland Press, 1983. Loyalist passenger lists.

Pioneer Profiles of New Brunswick Settlers. By Charlotte Gourlay Robinson. Pub. by Mika Pub. Co., Belleville, Ontario, 1980. Story about settlers to New Brunswick.

Early Families. Prepared by New Brunswick Genealogical Society, S. E. Branch, 1987. Listing of family genealogies.

Greener Pastures. By Earle Thomas. Pub. by Mika Pub., 1983. Story about a New York Loyalist family going to New Brunswick.

Early New Brunswick Probate Records 1785-1835. By R. Wallace Hale. Pub. by Heritage Books Inc., Bowie, MD, 1989.

The New Brunswick Militia Commissioned Officers' Visits 1787-1867. By David R. Facey-Crowther. Pub. by Capital Free Press, 1984.

The Envy of the American States: The Loyalist Dream for New Brunswick
By Ann Gorman Condon.

Over The Portage: Early History of the Upper Miramichi.
By William R. MacKinnon Jr. Pub. by New Ireland Press, New Brunswick, Canada.

Loyalists of New Brunswick.
By Esther Clark Wright, 1965. Pub. by author.

Kingston & the Loyalists of the Spring Fleet 1783.
By Walter Bates, 1980. Printed by Centennial Print & Litho LDT, New Brunswick.

Kiersteads of New Brunswick, Canada.
By Mrs. Martin Kierstead & Mr. Enoch Markham, 1973. Printed privately.

Loyalist Families.
By Cleadie Barnett & Elizabeth Sewell, 1983. Pub. by UEL, Fredericton, New Brunswick Branch.

Land Grants of Loyalists.
Series of land grant maps held at Dept. of Transportation, Fredericton, New Brunswick.

Quaker Loyalist Settlement in Pennfield, New Brunswick, 1783.
By J.M. Walton. Pub. by author, 1940.

Quaker Loyalist Settlers in New Brunswick & Nova Scotia.
By Dean of William Penn College.

Canada, Loyalists to: The 1783 Settlement of Quakers and Others at Passamaquoddy.
By Theodore C. Holmes. Pub. by Picton Press, 1993.
Has 6,602 people listed, many Loyalist lines.

The Saint John County Census 1851, 2 volumes.
By New Brunswick Provincial Archives, 1982.
Lists old surviving Loyalists.

The Story of Sussex & Vicinity.
By Grace Lybia Aiton. Pub. by Kings County Historical Society, New Brunswick, Canada, 1967.

The New Brunswick Museum Dept. of Canadian History Archives Division, Inventory of Manuscripts, 1967. Pub. by museum.

Diaries and Reminiscences of New Brunswick Women 1783-1980.
By Joanne Ritchie, 1997.

Harriet Irving Library, (Loyalist Studies)

University of New Brunswick
P.O. Box 7500
Fredericton, New Brunswick
Canada E3B 5H5
Phone: 506-453-4748
Internet Location: http://www.lib.unb.ca/collections/loyalist/

They have a very extensive Loyalist collection of printed materials, microfilm, etc.

Land Registration & Information Service

110 Charlotte Street, P.O. Box 5001
Saint John, New Brunswick
Canada E2L 4L4
Phone: 506-658-2419

This location carries early deeds and other records related to Saint John County and city.

Saint John Regional Library

Market Square Mall (2nd Floor)
Saint John, New Brunswick, Canada.

The following are some materials located at the library.

Newspapers: 1784 to the present.

Census of New Brunswick: 1851 (There are later census, but this will be the last showing Loyalists.

Custom House Port Returns: 1816, 1833, 1834, 1837, 1838.

Land Petitions: 1783-1857.

Marriage records: Dates vary by county.

Parish records: Dates vary by county.

Poll Books: Two counties only.

Probate records: Dates vary by county. Card and microfilm files on family genealogies.

Note: Many records and materials have been transferred at this location from the New Brunswick museum collection.

And More New Brunswick Locations

Kings County Historical and Archival Society, Inc., Kings County Museum, Centennial Building, Hampton, New Brunswick, Canada E0G 1Z0. They also have a newsletter.

The New Brunswick Historical Society, 120 Union St. (The Loyalist House), Saint John, New Brunswick, Canada E2L 1A3. This society is located in the oldest Loyalist house in Saint John. The house is open to the public. A National Historical Site, the Loyalist House was built by David Daniel Merritt, a United Empire Loyalist who came from New York. The house was completed in 1817. After four generations of Merritts living there, the house was bought by The New Brunswick Historical Society in 1959. Six generations have occupied this house at one time or another. A grand Georgian mansion, the Loyalist house is the finest in Saint John. It is opened to the public from June to September, weekdays, 10 AM to 5 PM.

Sundays are 1 PM to 5 PM. Free to members of the society which operates the house.

Note: Any New Brunswick parish records can be found at the Canadian National Archives which is listed in this book.

New Brunswick Internet Locations

Old & New Date To "WE LIVED" Newsletter
By Cleadie B. Barnett, Certified Genealogist
Years of research went into this massive collection of New Brunswick genealogy and sources. Much on Loyalists.
Website: http://genweb.net/~nbspast/

New Brunswick Genealogical Sites & Locations
Includes county sites too.
Website: http://www.inlandnet.com/~jveinot/cghl/new-brunswick.html

New Brunswick Family Site
By Ruby Cusack
She has included her multiple Loyalist lines in her site including vitals from newspapers and other sources. Includes query section.
http://personal.nbnet.nb.ca/rmcusack/

New Brunswick GenWeb Site
Website: http://www.bitheads.ca/nbgenweb/index.htm

QUEBEC

The Archives Nationales du Quebec

P.O. Box 10450
Saint-Foy, Quebec, Canada G1V 4N1
Phone: 418-644-4795

Census (pertain to Loyalist period)

1825: (Heads of household)
1831: (Heads of household)
1842: (Heads of household)
1851: (Lists entire family)

Parish Records

(See listing at National Archives of Canada located in this book)

Land Records

List of Crown grants dated 1763-1890.

Estate Records

These records can be found at each Court House in each district.

Genealogical & Historical Societies

Quebec Family History Society, P.O. Box 1026, Station Pointe Claire, Pointe Claire, Quebec, Canada H9S 4H9.
Website: http://www.cam.org/~qfhs/index.html
(This location may have loyalist records for the ones who settled southern Quebec)

Genealogy Society of Cantons, de l'Est, Case Postale 635, Sherbrooke, Quebec, Canada J1H 5K5.
(A prime Loyalist location for southern Quebec)

Loyalist Period Sites

Old Port of Quebec, Quebec City.

Fortifications of Quebec, Quebec City.

Missisquoi Museum (also known as the Loyalist Museum), Stanbridge East, Quebec.

Quebec Books & Research Guides

The Loyalists of Quebec 1774-1825, A Forgotten History. By Heritage Branch of UEL, 1989. A history of Quebec Loyalists.

Quebec Montreal and Ottawa. By T. Morris Longstreth. Pub. by The Century Co., NY & London, 1933. A history of that area.

Note: Today's figures stand at 10,000 Loyalists who settled in Quebec, mostly in the southern region, and around Sherbrooke/Lennoxville area just north of the New Hampshire/Vermont border.

Quebec Internet Locations

Quebec GenWeb Page
Website: http://www.cam.org/~beaur/qcgenweb.html

Quebec Eastern Townships & New England Genealogy
Website: http://www.virtuel.qc.ca/simmons/

Eastern Township Research Page
Website: http://www.geocities.com/Heartland/Acres/3500/et.html

ONTARIO

The Archives of Ontario

77 Grenville Street West
Quenn's Park, Toronto,
Ontario, Canada M7A 2R9
Phone: 416-965-4030

Census (pertain to Loyalist period)

1842: (Heads of household)
1848: (Heads of household)
1850: (Heads of household)
1851: (Lists all family members)

Land Records

Copies of land titles can be obtained from the Recording Office, Ministry of Government Services, 3rd floor, Hearst Block, Queen's Park, Toronto, Ontario, Canada M7A 1N3. (Please note that all Loyalists were not issued a recorded grant).

Estate Records

These archives hold indexed files of Court of Probate records from 1791 to 1859.

Surrogate Court records on microfilm from 1793 to 1900.

Loyalists Period Sites & Museums

(Ontario has many Loyalists sites. These are only a few).

Fort Mississauga

Fort George

Fort Niagara

Butler's Barracks

Killman Art Gallery
237 Unity Rd. E.
R.R. #1
Caledonia, Ontario
Canada N0A 1A0
Phone: 416-765-4261

Murray Killman U.E., is the owner and artist of nature paintings of scarce and endangered animals, but he also specializes in Loyalist art. Being a descendant of Lt. Colonel John Butler, U. E. (1725-1796). He recreates scenes from the Loyalist period on canvas and on collector plates. His work is of the highest quality and is recognized by the United Empire Loyalist Association of Canada. Privately, he owns many exotic pets from around the world.

Simcoe's Eva Brook Donly Museum

Simcoe, Ontario

Contains a large library on material on the local history and volumes of family genealogies. It is run by the Norfolk Historical Society. The archives there is excellent.

Loyalist Cultural Center and Museum

Adolphustown U.E. Loyalist Park
Adolphustown, Ontario,
Canada
Website: http://genweb.net/~boquel/

Operated by the UEL, Bay of Quinte Branch.
Has Loyalist artifacts, exhibits and a genealogy library. This is the site of the Loyalist landing on 16 June 1784. It also includes a Loyalist cemetery which was restored in 1956

Ontario Societies for Loyalist Study

Ontario Genealogical Society
Box 66 Station Q
Toronto, Ontario,
Canada M4T 2L7.
Website: http://www.ogs.on.ca/
This society has many branches located all over the province. Their newsletter is an excellent one. They hold conferences and lectures and are extremely active.

Canadian Historical Association, 395 Wellington St., Ottawa, Ontario, Canada K1A 0N3

Heraldry Society of Canada, 125 Lakeway Dr., Ottawa, Ontario, Canada K1I 5A9.
(The only institution outside England allowed to award crests to organizations, individuals and towns, etc.)

United Empire Loyalists' Association of Canada, The George Brown House, 50 Baldwin St., Toronto, Ontario, Canada M5T 1L4 (Listed by itself in this book)

Ontario Historical Society, 1466 Bathurst St., Toronto, Ontario, Canada M5R 3J3

The British Isles Family History Society of Greater Ottawa
Box 38026
Ottawa, Ontario,
Canada K2C 1N0
They offer a diskette with 3,200 websites in British Isles, North America, Australia and New Zealand.

UEL, Bay of Quinte Branch
Adolphustown, Ontario, Canada
A very active branch since 1956. See the above Loyalist Cultural Center and Museum.
Website: http://genweb.net/~boquel/

Note: There were over 10,000 Loyalists who settled in Ontario. This area was also called Upper Canada.

Loyalist Book/Gazettes Outlets

Global Genealogy Supply
13 Charles St.
Milton, Ontario,
Canada L9T 2G5
Phone: 800-361-5168 or 905-875-2176
Internet Location: http://globalgenealogy.com/list32.htm

Rick Roberts sells books and materials for genealogy research. He produces *The Global Gazette* on the internet http://globalgenealogy.com/gazed26.htm Articles and genealogy news is of the highest quality and interest to the Loyalists researcher.

Ontario Books & Guides

Pioneer Life on the Bay of Quinte.
Pub. by Mika Pub. Co., Belleville, Ontario, 1983.

Ontarian Families. By Edward Chadwick. Pub. by Hunterdon House, Lambertville, NJ, 2nd Printing 1983. Stories and genealogies of families in Ontario.

The Settlement of Upper Canada. By William Canniff. Pub. by Mika Pub., 1983. A History of Ontario and its people.

The Loyalists in Ontario. By William D. Reid. Pub. by Hunterdon House, NJ 1973. Lists of Loyalists.

The Loyal Americans: The military Role of the Loyalist Provincial Corps and Their Settlement in British North America 1775-84. By Robert S. Allen. Pub. by The Canadian War Museum, 1983.

Index-Baptisms & Marriages: Brockville & District 1812-1848. By Edwin A Livingston C.D., U.E., 1985.

Early Methodist Records. By the Bay of Quinte Branch of the UEL, 1986.

Victorious in Defeat: The Loyalists in Canada. By Wallace Brown & Hereward Dr. Pub. by Methuen Pub., Toronto, Ontario 1984.

An Early Ontario Harvest. By Helen & Marguerite Dow. Pub. by Osgoode Township Historical Society. Collections of recipes, date unknown.

United Empire Loyalists – Pioneers of Upper Canada
By Nick & Helma Mika, 1976
A History.

King's Men: The Soldier Founders of Ontario
By Mary Beacock Fryer (date and publisher not listed).

From Loyal Township to Industrial City: Cornwall, 1784-1984
By Elinor Kyte Sr. Pub. by Mika Pub. Co., Belleville, Ontario, 1983.

An Enduring Heritage: Black Contributions to Early Ontario.
By Roger Riendeau. Pub. by Dundurn Press, 1984.

Loyalists of Ontario, Sons and Daughters of American Loyalists of Upper Canada.
By W.D. Reid. Pub. by Hunterdon House, NJ, 1973.

Centennial of Settlements of Upper Canada
By UEL, 1784-1884. Pub. by Gregg Press, 1972.

Genealogical Sources at Archives of Ontario.
By Ontario Archives, Toronto, Ontario, Canada, 1979.

Loyalist Narratives from Upper Canada.
By J.J. Talman. Pub. by Greenwood Press, 1970.

Loyalist Families of the Grand River Branch, United Empire Loyalists' Association of Canada.
Pub. by Pro Familia Pub., 1991

Loyalist Internet Locations & Sources

Loyalists Genealogy (Ontario)
By Edward Kipp
http://www.magma.ca/~ekipp

Ontario GenWeb Page
Website: http://www.multiboard.com/~sperrit/ongenweb/

Guide to Genealogical Resources in Stauffer Library
Website: http://130.15.161.74/inforef/guides/genealogy.htm

Ontario Cemetery Finding Aid
Website: http://www.islandnet.com/oefa

Ontario Vital Statistics
Website: gopher://ftp.cac.psu.edu:70/00/genealogy/text/guides/ontvtl91

Bruce County Genealogical Society
Website: http://www.compunik.com/vmall/begs/

Kingston Branch, Ontario Genealogical Society
Website: http://post.queensu.ca/~murduckb/kgbrogs.htm

Lambton Branch, Ontario Genealogical Society
Website: http://www.sarnia.com/groups/ogs/lambton_page.html

Waterloo-Wellington Branch, Ontario Genealogical Society
Website: http://www.des.uwaterloo.ca/~marj/genealogy/ww.html

Waterloo Historical Society
Website: http://www.des.uwaterloo.ca/~marj/history/whs.html

Wellington County Historical Society
Website: http://www.des.uwaterloo.ca/~marj/history/wellington.html

Wainfleet Township Public Library
Website: http://st-cath.ont.net/wainfleet/library/wtpl.htm

Wainfleet Township Public Library Genealogy Page
Website: http://st-cath.ont.net/wainfleet/library/genmain.htm

Ontario Loyalist Cemeteries

Carl-Misener-Bald Cemetery
Carl Street
Port Robinson, Ontario, Canada

Location: Carl street is located on the west side of the Welland Canal at Port Robinson. From St. Catherines follow highway 406 toward Welland. Just before Welland, take a left turn onto Port Robinson Road and follow the canal. Carl Street is on the right. Follow parking directions. A few stones are still standing. The Misener, Carl and Bald families are buried there, all from Loyalist lines.

MANITOBA

The Provincial Archives of Manitoba

200 Vanghan Street
Winnipeg, Manitoba, Canada R3C 1P5
Phone: 204-944-3971
Website: http://www.gov.mb.ca/che/archives/index.html

Census (There could be mention of Loyalists who may have immigrated west early)

1832: (Heads of household)
1834: (Heads of household)
1835: (Heads of household)
1849: (Heads of household)
1843: (Heads of household)
1846: (Heads of household)
1849: (Heads of household)

Genealogical Societies

The Manitoba Genealogical Society, P.O. Box 2066, Winnipeg, Manitoba, Canada R3C 3R4

Historical Societies

Manitoba Historical Society, 314 – 63 Albert St., Winnipeg, Manitoba, Canada R3B 1G4. Phone: 204-947-0559.

Manitoba Internet Locations

Hudson Bay Company Archives
Website: http://www.gov.mb.ca/chc/archives/hbca/index.html

Manitoba Public Library Links (English)
Website: http://pls.chc.gov.ca:8080/pls/web_sites.html

Guides for Genealogical Research
Website: http://www.gov.mb.ca/leg-lib/webfam.html

Manitoba GenWeb Page
Website: http://www.rootsweb.com/~canmb/index.htm

Note: There is not much information in this province regarding land grants because no Loyalist grants were given to the western territories.

SASKATCHEWAN

Saskatchewan Archives Board

Regina Office/University of Regina
Regina, Saskatchewan, Canada S4S 0A2
Phone: 306-787-4068

Societies

Saskatchewan Genealogical Society
2nd Floor, 1870 Lorne Street
P.O. Box 1894
Regina, Saskatchewan,
Canada S4P 3E1
Phone: 306-780-9207
Fax: 306-781-6021
Website: http://wwwsaskgenealogy.com/

Saskatchewan Internet Locations

Saskatchewan GenWeb Page
Website: http://www.rootsweb.com/~cansk/Saskatchewan/

Saskatchewan Provincial Library
Website: telnet://PROVLIB.GOV.SK.CA:23
Login: Public

Saskatoon Public Library
Website: http://www.public.asakatoon.sk.ca/
Login: Public, then type PAC. To exit, type Quit at both prompts.

Note: There are no Loyalist materials here except for holdings given from outside the area. There could be mention of Loyalist ancestors of Saskatchewan settlers.

ALBERTA

Provincial Archives of Alberta

12845 – 102 Avenue
Edmonton, Alberta, Canada T5N 0M6
Phone: 403-427-1750

Alberta Internet Locations

Alberta GenWeb Page
Website:
http://www.geocities.com/Heartland/Hills/3508/albertagenweb.html

Alberta Family Histories Society
Website: http://www.calcna.ab.ca/afhs/

Genealogy in Edmonton, Alberta
Website: http://www.freenet.edmonton.ab.ca/famhist/

Lethbridge Family History Center – Alberta Genealogy Library
Website: http://www.leth.net/fhe/

Note: There are no Loyalist records here except for imported ones or those mentioned in genealogies of some settlers.

Societies

The Alberta Genealogical Society
Prince of Wales Armouries Heritage Center
#116, 10440 – 108 Ave.
Edmonton, Alberta,
Canada T5H 3Z9
Phone: 780-424-4429
Fax: 780-423-8980
E-mail: agsoffice@compusmart.ab.ca
(Also on the internet)

Note: There are many branches located throughout the province.

BRITISH COLUMBIA

Provincial Archives of British Columbia

655 Belleville Street
Victoria, British Columbia, Canada V8V 1X4
Phone: 604-387-5885 or 604-387-1952
Website: http://www.bcarchives.gov.bc.ca/index.htm

Note: There are no Loyalist materials here except for the imported records from the eastern province or family genealogies from western settlers.

The United Empire Loyalists' Association of Canada

The Victoria Branch
1825 Quamicham Ave.
Victoria, British Columbia
Canada V8S 2B4
Internet Location: http://www.npiec.on.ca/~uela/uelal.htm
E-mail Address: uela@npiec.on.ca

In 1985 this branch published *The Loyalist Gazette Index: 1963-1985*. A great help to locating surnames that were listed in all 1000 pages of the gazettes.

Societies

British Columbia Genealogy Society
Box 88054
Lansdowne Mall
Richmond, British Columbia,
Canada V6X 3T6
Phone: 604-502-9119
Fax: 604-263-4952
E-mail: bcgs@npsnet.com
(They are also on the internet)

British Columbia Historical Association
3450 West 20th Ave.
Vancouver, British Columbia
Canada

(The above societies have lists of other societies in the area)

British Columbia Internet Locations

British Columbia GenWeb Page
Website: http://www.islandnet.com/~jveinot/genweb/begenweb.html

British Columbia Cemetery Finding Aid
Website: http://www.islandnet.com/beefa/homepage.html

YUKON TERRITORY

The Yukon Archives

P.O. Box 2703
Whitehorse, Yukon Territory, Canada Y1A 2C6
Phone: 403-667-5321

Societies

Yukon Historical Society
Whitehorse, Yukon Territory
Canada

Dawson City Museum and Historical Society
P.O. Box 303
Dawson City, Yukon
Canada Y0B 1G0
Phone: 403-993-5291
Fax: 403-993-5839
E-mail: dcmuseum@yknet.yk.ca (or) can-dcm@immedia.ca

Note: There are no Loyalist records here except for the imported ones from the eastern provinces, and family genealogies of westward settlers.

Yukon Internet Locations

Yukon GenWeb Site
Website: http://www.rootsweb.com/~canyk/

Yukon & Alaska History Page
Includes a genealogy hook-up under Resources.
Website: http://yukonalaska.miningco.com

NORTHWEST TERRITORIES

The Archives of the Northwest Territories

Prince of Wales Northern Heritage Center
Yellowknife, Northwest Territories
Canada X1A 2L9
Phone: 404-873-7698
Website: http://pwnhe.learnnet.nt.ca/programs/archives.htm

Societies

The NWT Genealogical Society
P.O. Box 1715
Yellowknife, NWT
Canada X1A 2P3
Phone: 867-873-5424 (as of 1999, Linda Whitford, President)

Note: There are no Loyalist records here except for the imported materials from the eastern provinces, and family genealogies of westward settlers.

THE UNITED EMPIRE LOYALISTS' ASSOCIATION OF CANADA

Dominion Headquarters
The George Brown House
50 Baldwin St.
Toronto, Ontario, Canada M5T 1L4

This excellent society has branches in every province of Canada. Loyalist ancestors are registered and descendants are honored with the "U.E." initials after their surnames signifying their connection to their Loyalist ancestor. Each pedigree must be proven by documentation.

The Loyalist Gazette is their magazine, which comes out twice per year. Filled with colorful pictures and excellent articles on all ethnic groups of the Loyalists, and any historical facts of interest.

The term U.E. "United Empire Loyalists" came about on Monday, 9 November 1789 when Sir Guy Carleton, Lord Dorchester, Governor-General of Canada, intimated to his Executive Council "that it was his wish to put a Marke of Honour upon the families who had adhered to the unity of the Empire, and joined the Royal Standard in America before the Treaty of Separation in the year 1783." The council agreed and ordered that several Land Boards prepare a registry of persons who persevered in their loyalty to the Crown at great sacrifice to themselves. This created the "Old U.E.L." list, which has been added to up to this day. Each person proving descent from a Loyalist ancestor is entitled to the letters "U.E." after his or her surname. This must be done after the United Empire Loyalists" Association reviews and approves the documentation proving descent.

Each year this organization has a convention in one of the Canadian provinces. New officers are chosen, and various speakers appear, and events take place over a two or three day period. In 1989, His Majesty The Prince Philip was the honored guest to celebrate the anniversary of the Lord Dorchester accord of 1789.

Various U.E.L. Items of Interest

The United Empire Loyalists' Museum
Adolphustown Provincial Park
Loyalist Parkway, Ontario, Canada

Hours: 10 A.M. to 5 P.M. (every day except Saturday and Monday from mid-June to Labour Day).

For special visits contact the director at:
Box 215
Bloomfield, Ontario,
Canada K0K 1G0

This is a UEL museum once owned by David W. Allison in Adolphustown. This is a three-story home built in 1878 and contains Loyalist artifacts along with a library of Loyalist books and records. (The Loyalist House located in Saint John, New Brunswick is another fine Loyalist house and museum, operated by the New Brunswick Historical Society).

The United Empire Loyalists' Commemorative Stamp

Issued on 3 July 1984, this stamp features a group of Loyalists dressed in eighteenth-century clothing. In the background is the Grand Union flag, the British flag used from 1606 to 1801 (Also called "The Queen Ann's flag). The stamp was designed by Will Davies, an illustrator from Toronto, Canada. The denomination is thirty-two cents. Available through collectors now.

Books Published by the UEL

Loyal She Remains. Pub. by UEL of Canada, Toronto, Canada, 1988. A pictorial history commemorating the bicentennial of Ontario. More than 690 pages of history and over 1000 illustrations. Order from the main branch.

History of Loyalist Associations in Canada

Loyalist Lineages of Canada 1783-1983.
By UEL, Toronto Branch, Pub. by Generation Press, 1984.

Loyalist Lineages, Vols. I & II
Pub. by UEL
Genealogy listing of all members and family between 1971-1989 to their Loyalist.

Family History of Loyalists & Their Descendants Index of the Non-Lending Library.
By UEL.

Association History

The United Empire Loyalists' Association of Canada was incorporated by an Act of Parliament on May 27, 1914. Other Loyalist associations from the past were:

New Brunswick:
The Loyal Refugee Association, 1846
The New Brunswick Loyalist Society, 1889

Nova Scotia:
The United Empire Loyalists' Association of Nova Scotia, 1897.

Quebec:
The United Empire Loyalist's Association of Montreal, 1896.

Ontario:
The United Empire Loyalists' Association of Ontario, 1896.

Alberta:
The Loyalist Association, 1913.

In today's association the following rules apply to qualify for membership:

Either male or female; as of April 19, 1775, a resident of the American Colonies, and joined the Royal Standard prior to the Treaty of Separation of 1783, or otherwise demonstrated loyalty to the Crown, and settled in territory remaining under the rule of the Crown.

or

a soldier who served in an American Loyalist Regiment and was disbanded in Canada.

or

a member of the Six Nations Indians of either the Grand River or Bay of Quiete Reserve, or from other migrations that were associated with the Loyalists.

Georgia, New York and South Carolina were Loyalist strongholds, followed by New Jersey, Massachusetts, Maryland, and Rhode Island, etc. New York had produced more forces than all the other colonies combined. There were 312 companies in fifty different Provincial Corps with the American Loyalists taking part in every major battle throughout the war.

After the war, these very gallant people had to migrate to the following locations:

The United Kingdom
The Bahamas
Sierra Leone
Jamaica
Canada
Florida
Dominica
St. Vincent

Roughly four million Canadians are descendants of Loyalists, not to forget their Australian brothers who immigrated there from Canada during the settlement of that continent in the mid-to late 1800's. Many were recorded in the famous prisoner colonies.

Loyalist claims amounted to over 4,118 people and totaled over $200 million dollars, a fraction of over the reported 100,000 Loyalists who had to leave the Colonies.

UEL Branches

Maritimes:

Halifax, Dartmouth Branch, Nova Scotia
Fredericton Branch, New Brunswick
Saint John Branch, New Brunswick
Abegweit Branch, Prince Edward Island

Quebec:

Heritage Branch, Montreal, Quebec
Sir John Johnson, Quebec
Little Forks Branch, Lennoxville, Quebec

Ontario:

Sir Guy Carleton Branch, Ottawa, Ontario
St. Lawrence Branch, Cornwall, Morrisburg, and Eastern Ontario
Col. Edward Jessop Branch, Brockville and area
Kingston and District Branch

Bay of Quinte Branch, Adolphustown, Napanee, Picton, Belleville and area.
Toronto Branch
Governor Simcoe Branch, Totonto
Costume Branch
Hamilton Branch
Col. John Butler (Niagara) Branch
Bicentennial Branch (Windsor area)
Grand River Branch (Kitchener, Brantford, Simcoe areas)
London and Western Ontario Branch

Prairie Provinces:
Manitoba Branch
Regina Saskatchewan Branch
Edmonton Alberta Branch
Calgary Alberta Branch

Western Canada:
Vancouver British Columbia Branch
Chilliwack Branch
Thompson, Okanagan Branch
Victoria Branch

The Canadian Heraldic Authority

Chief Heraldic of Canada
Canadian Heraldic Authority Rideau Hall
Ottawa, Ontario, Canada K1A 0A1
Phone: 613-991-2227

On 4 June 1988, His Royal Highness The Prince Edward presented Letters Patent to Her Excellency the Governor General that authorizes the creation of the Canadian Heraldic Authority. This mechanism was created to empower the Governor General of Canada to exercise the granting of arms. This office's major duties will include:

Petitions for new grants of arms;

Registration of new grants and of existing arms, flags and badges;

Registration of native symbols;

Registration of genealogical information related to inheritance of arms;

Provision of information on correct heraldic practice;

Provision of information on heraldic artists related to graphic or architectural projects and manufactured products.

This authority was given the right to bestow arms to all registered United Empire Loyalists, but when this author tried to register my loyalist ancestor, I was denied because I was an American citizen. They never said no, but they instructed me that they were looking into the matter because the person being honored was a loyalist. Presently, they still discriminate against American loyalist descendants honoring their loyalists ancestors; something I hope will change in the future.

Internet Sources For Canadian Records & Loyalist Materials

FAQ For Canadian Military Genealogy
Website: http://www.ott.igs.net/~donpark/canmilfaq.htm

National Library of Canada
Is listed in French & English, all libraries in Canada.
Website: http://www.nle-bne.ca

Canadian Military Records
Website: ftp://ftp.cac.psu.edu/pub/genealogy/text/guides/can-mil.txt

Canadian Vital Records
Website: ftp://ftp.cac.psu.edu/pub/genealogy/text/guides/can-vitl.txt

Canadian Genealogy Books
Website: ftp://ftp.cac.psu.edu/pub/genealogy/text/guides/can-book.txt

Canadian Roots
By Lori Fox – Loyalist Interests
http://www.ingenas.com

3 *U.S.A.*

WASHINGTON, D.C.

The National Archives

National Archives and Records Service
General Services Administration
Washington DC 20408

National Branch
Phone: 202-501-5400
Website: http://www.nara.gov:80/ http://gopher.nara.gov/
http://www.nara.gov/nara/del/dcarca.html
http://www.nara.gov/genealogy/
US Military Records: http://www.flash.net/~mccphys/cw.htm

The following branches are the extensions of the national branch of the archives. There are regional branches throughout the United States, but listed here are only the areas pertaining to the American Revolution. This does not mean there are no revolutionary records at those other locations, so for those with travel problems, you can check the other branches in Chicago, Kansas City, Fort Worth, Denver, Los Angeles, San Francisco, and Seattle.

Boston Branch

380 Trapelo Rd., Waltham, MA 02154. Phone: 617-647-8100. This branch serves Connecticut, Maine, Massachusetts, New Hampshire, Rhode Island and Vermont.
(Some records may be placed at an annex branch so check before going there)

New York Branch

Building 22-M.O.T. Bayonne St., Bayonne, NJ 07002. Phone: 201-823-7545.
This branch serves New York, New Jersey, Puerto Rico, New York, and The Virgin Islands.

Philadelphia Branch

5000 Wissahickon Ave., Philadelphia, PA 19144. Phone: 215-951-5591. This branch serves Delaware, Pennsylvania, Maryland, Virginia, and West Virginia.

Atlanta Branch

1557 St. Joseph Ave., East Point, GA 30344. Phone: 404-763-7477. This branch serves Alabama, Georgia, Florida, Kentucky, Mississippi, North Carolina, South Carolina, and Tennessee.

The following records are located at the archives and some can be requested from other branches. You must inquire first. (Some of the records may be Patriot, but many Loyalists were once Patriots who changed sides later on).

Revolutionary War Rolls dated 1775-1783

Connecticut, Adjutant General's Office. *Record of Service of Connecticut Men in the Revolutionary War.* By Connecticut Historical Society, Vols. 8 and 12.

Delaware Public Archives Commission. By Delaware Archives. Vols. 1-3.

Georgia, Department of Archives and History. Georgia's Roster of the Revolution. Pages 374-435.

Maryland Historical Society. Archives of Maryland. Vol. 18.

Massachusetts, Secretary of the Commonwealth. Massachusetts Soldiers and Sailors of the Revolutionary War (Do not forget Maine in this material).

New Hampshire, Isaac Weare Hammond, Rolls of the Soldiers in the Revolutionary War. (Could be listed as Provincial and State Papers, vols. 14-17).

New Jersey, Adjutant General's Office. Official Register of the Officers and Men of New Jersey in the Revolutionary War. (With index).

New York (State) University. Documents Relating to the Colonial History of the State of New York, vol. 15.

New York, Comptroller's Office. New York in the Revolution as County and State, vol. I.
North Carolina. The State Records of North Carolina, vol. 16.

Pennsylvania Archives, 2nd Series, vols. 10, 11, 13-15; 3rd series, vol. 23; 5th series, vols. 1-8; 6th series, vols. 1-2 (General index).

Vermont. Rolls of the Soldiers in the Revolutionary War.

Virginia, John H. Gwathmey. Historical Register of Virginians in the Revolution; Soldiers, Sailors, Marines.

Virginia, State Library, Department of Archives and History. List of Revolutionary Soldiers of Virginia.

A card list of Volunteer Soldiers arranged by state can be found at the National Archives Building. Compiled by type of records found: muster rolls, returns, hospital registers, prison records and other records. Each card is arranged by state, under military unit and then alphabetically by name. Many original records were destroyed by fire on 8 November 1800 and during the British attack on Washington D.C. in 1814.

Pictures of Tories for sale at the Archives

Joseph Brant (Thayendanegea) (Native Loyalist). Drawing (3/4 length) from painting by Romney, 1774 (#111-SC-92608).

John Burgoyne. Engraving (Bust) by S. Hollyer (#148-GW-616).

Marquis Cornwallis. Engraving (Full length) by J. Ward from painting by Sir W. Beechey; Published in 1799 (#148-GW-463).

Thomas Gage. Engraving (Bust) (#111-SC-94745).

King George III of England. Mezzotint (3/4 length) by E. Fisher from painting by Benjamin West; Published in 1778 (#148-GW-473).

William Phillips. Engraving (Bust) (#111-SC-92594).

Baron Friedrich Riedesel. Painting (bust) by Schroeder. (#111-SC-92607).

Baroness Riedesel. Painting (1/2 length) by Tischbein. (#111-SC-92568).

Barry St. Leger. Engraving (bust) from miniature by R. Cosway. (#111-SC-92625).

Banastre Tarleton. Painting (full length) by Sir Joshua Reynolds, c. 1782. (#148-GW-619).

Benedict Arnold. Etching (bust profile) by H.B. Hall, 1879 (#148-GW-617).

Charles Lee. Engraving (1/2 length) by G.R. Hall (#148-GW-632).

Peggy Shippen (Mrs. Benedict Arnold) and child (seated pose). Painting by Sir Thomas Lawrence (#111-SC-92575).

Sizes available are: 8X10, 11X14, 16X20.

Order from: Cashier, National Archives (GSA), Washington, D.C. 20408.

Library of Congress

General Reading Rooms Division
Thomas Jefferson Building Rm. 244
Washington, D.C. 20408
Phone: 202-707-5000

The staff here does not do searches, but the library is open to the public, and many titles can go out on interlibrary loan. Nearly every book written on the Loyalists can be found here. The holdings at this location are too large to list.

Genealogical & Historical Societies Located in Washington DC

American Society of Genealogists
Box 4970, Washington, DC 20008

American Historical Association
4000 A Street SE,
Washington, DC 20003

The Hereditary Order of Descendants of The Loyalists and Patriots of The American Revolution

Present Governor General, Mrs. Donald Cecil Trolinger
(Address changes when office changes)
Ottawa Hill, Route 1, Box 154
Miami, OK 74354-9370
918-542-5772

This organization is the only Loyalist society located in the United States. Each year they have a convention in Washington D.C. usually planned around Patriots Day. Their by-laws state that the speaker must always speak about Loyalists. They were founded approximately in 1973.

Newsletter

The Crown and Eagle

Excellent newsletter listing events, society business, and Loyalist ancestors of members who were approved by the board as proven descendants. The listing gives a short history of each Loyalist. It also includes member lists and who their Patriot/Loyalists were, making it easy for contact.

Holdings

They have a library consisting of donated and purchased books, including reproduction projects of the *Crown & Eagle* for other libraries.

Other Addresses

This society shares space with the District of Columbia S.A.R. at 2025 Eye Street, N.W. Washington, D.C.

State Locations

The following states, consisting of all thirteen colonies, and Florida, were involved in the American Revolution. Each lost some portion of its population to the Loyalist cause. Records pertaining only to Loyalists are listed here, but keep in mind that other records may list your Loyalist ancestor. More material is made available to all the other states as well.

CONNECTICUT

Connecticut State Library

Archives History & Genealogy Unit
231 Capitol Ave., Hartford, CT 06106

This site has the most extensive collection in the state.

Vital Records – The Barbour Collection is the most desired source containing births, marriages and deaths up to 1850.

Church Records – Containing over 600 church records dating back to the seventieth century.

Family Bible Records – Nearly 25,000 entries from Bibles in 26 volumes.

Newspapers – Taken from 90 early papers dating from 1750 to 1870, contained in bound volumes.

Probate Records – Copies of original records prior to 1850. Also available on microfilm.

Special Collections – Many unindexed collections.

Military Records – Many records dating as far back as 1635.

Court Records – A very large collection of court records dated to 1855.

The Charles R. Hale Collection – This is a supplement to the Barbour Collection.

Revolutionary documents, pay rolls, orderly books, etc.

Superior Court records to 1796.

Many large collections of private genealogical material donated to the library.

Societies in Connecticut

The Connecticut Society of Genealogists, Inc.
2906 Main Street
P.O. Box 435
Glastonbury, CT 06033

The Connecticut Historical Society

The Middlesex County Historical Society
Middletown, CT 06457

Fairfield Historical Society

The New London Historical Society
New London, CT

Other Records in Connecticut

Many towns have vital records up through 1850

Each town houses its own land records.

Military records are also kept at the town level, but the state archives has published works.

Some church records are still located at the churches in their towns.

Connecticut Books and Materials

Bailey's Early Connecticut Marriages, 7 volumes. Pub. by Genealogical Pub. Co., 1976. Reprint of 1896 edition. Marriages records before 1800.

Colonial Records of Connecticut (1635-1776). 15 volumes. Publisher & author not found, but copy is located at the Connecticut State Library, listed under Connecticut archives.

French and Indian War Muster Rolls & Revolutionary War. 2 volumes each. By The Connecticut Historical Society (date unknown).

The Traitor And The Spy. By James Flexner. Pub. by Harcourt, Brace and Co., New York, 1953. Story about Benedict Arnold, including his life in his home state of Connecticut.

The Battle of Groton Heights. By Charles Allyn, 1882, New London, CT. Loyalist attack on Fort Griswold, CT 6 Sept. 1781.

September 6, 1781, North Groton's Story. By Carolyn Smith and Helen Vergason. Pub. by A Printing Co., New London, CT 1984. A story about the American Loyalist attack on New London and Fort Griswold which was directed by Benedict Arnold.

Thunder Over New England, Benjamin Bonnell, The Loyalist. By Paul J. Bunnell, FACG, UE. Pub. by Christopher Pub., Hanover, MA 1988. A full account of the attack on New London and Fort Griswold on 6 September 1781 by the Loyalists and Benedict Arnold.

Loyalists of Connecticut.
By E. Peck. Pub. by Yale University Press, 1934.

Connecticut Loyalists: An Analysis of Loyalist Land Confiscation's in Greenwich, Stamform(sic) and Norwalk.
By John W. Tyler, New Orleans, 1977.

MAINE

This state was part of Massachusetts until 1820, so many records can be found in the Massachusetts Archives. From 1780 to 1820 Massachusetts administrated over this area, but it was called the District of Maine. This state existed as an independent province under the Gorges Patent granted by Charles I from 1677 to 1780, but governed by the Commonwealth of Massachusetts.

Maine State Archives

State House Station 84
Augusta, ME 04333
Phone: 207-289-2451

Military Records – Before 1820, can be obtained from the Archives of the Commonwealth of Massachusetts located at Columbia Point, Dorchester, MA. The Maine Archives does have militia rolls of men who served in the war of 1812.

Other Collections – The archives contains other material from Canada and Great Britain.

Newspapers – Some papers from other areas donated from other societies.

Court Records – (Only pertaining to Loyalist period). Cumberland County 1768–1929 (partially microfilmed); Lincoln County 1761–1899 (on microfilm); York County 1636–1929.

Records of the Municipal Courts (1825-1961) are in the custody of this institution.

The Old Circuit Court of Common Pleas contains information such as daily activities, various circumstances, occupations and many concerns of the citizens. Court was held in every county for jury trials and other law matters from 1780 to 1800.

Maine Eastern Lands Papers

These records are held at The Massachusetts Archives located at Columbia Point, Dorchester, MA. These are probably the most valuable records for the Loyalist period. Records can be called up by box numbers.

Box 1 – Accounts dated 1785-1794.

Box 2 – Accounts dated 1795-1833.

Box 8 – Applications for land, dated 1786-1853.

Box 9 – Bonds, Contracts, Permits, Copies of Resolves relating to Eastern Lands dated 1784-1853, and some undated records.

Box 10 – Various papers relating to the towns of Bakerstown, Belmont, Beauchamp, Leverett Claim, Bridgeton, Buckstown, East and West Butterfield, Foxcroft, Hartford, Hiram, New Canaan, Pejepscot, Phillips, Gore, Porterfield, Searsmont and Sumner dated 1786-1820.

Box 12 – Papers relating to the Eastern Boundary between the U.S. (Colonies) and Great Britain (Canada) dated 1765-1798.

Box 14 – Papers relating to Islands on the coast and lands east of the Penobscot River dated 1763-1853.

Box 17 – Various Letters dated 1783-1795.

(Note: There are many other boxes containing letters dated from 1793 to 1856).

Other records concerning the Eastern Lands. Committees and agents appointed by the General Court from 1781-1801.

Chapter 164 – Resolves of 1783, passed March 20, 1784. Committee of Cotton Tufts, Edward Russell and John Hill to depose of lands in York County (This does not necessarily mean there are Loyalists listed here whose property was taken by the state. There are many more chapters listed here but may or may not be of importance to the Loyalist researcher. Names may be given).

The Maine State Library

Cultural Building
Augusta, ME 04333
Phone: 207-289-3561

There is a large collection that covers the state, Canada, and Great Britain, but keep in mind, pre-1820 records are housed at the Massachusetts Archives unless extracted recently. The records that can be found here are:

State, county and town histories.

Published vital records.

Cemetery records and epitaphs, early church records.

Wills, deeds, general court and probate records, town and province records.

Pension lists, military rosters and regiment histories.

Indexes, dictionaries and bibliographies.

A surname index conducted by the Maine Old Cemetery Association.

Individual and collective genealogies and family histories, biographical collections pertaining to Maine and other states.

French-Canadian records of neighboring provinces (could show inter-marriages with Loyalists).

D.A.R. and other hereditary patriotic organizations, publications, records, rosters and histories.

Miscellaneous microfilm material pertaining to Maine history and genealogy.

Maine Societies

Maine Historical Society
Cultural Building
Augusta, ME 04333

Note: Many Maine records were destroyed by fire in various counties.

RHODE ISLAND

Division of Vital Statistics

Providence Dept. of Health
Kennedy Plaza
Providence, RI 02908
Phone: 401-421-7740, ext. 326 or 327
or

Rhode Island Secretary of State
Archives Division
Room 43, State House
Smith Street
Providence, RI 02903

This department contains all original birth, marriages and death documents dating from 1636 to 1981. (They do charge for copies).

Indexes are not accessible to public. Special projects may be granted to certified genealogists.

Rhode Island Societies and Libraries

Providence Public Library
150 Empire Street
Providence, RI 02903
Phone: 401-521-7722

They have census records of 1774, 1777 and 1782. The 1777 census was a military census, but it is not complete because part of this state was occupied by the British.

The Newport Historical Society
Newport, RI 02840

The pre-Revolutionary Newport Town records were carried off by the Tory town clerk in 1779, but the vessel carrying these records was sunk while trying to escape to New York City which was the British stronghold throughout the war. Years later, the ship was raised and some records were found, cleaned and mounted on silk, and returned to Newport.

Rhode Island Historical Society
c/o Providence Public Library
150 Empire St.
Providence, RI 02903

They have a very good revolutionary war collection.

Other Rhode Island Records

Providence Court House, Providence, RI has records dated 1730 to 1818.

Land records are at each town hall.

There are only five counties to research: Bristol, Kent, Newport, Providence, and Washington.

Probate, deeds and other town records can be found at each town or county court house.

Rhode Island Books and Materials

Vital Records of Rhode Island 1636-1850. Vols. 1-21. By James N. Arnold. The first series covers births, marriages and deaths, a family register for the people. Pub. by Narragansett Historical Pub. Co., 1891. Reprinted by New England Historical Genealogical Society, Boston, MA 1980.

The American Genealogist. By Ruth Wilder Sherman. (Was printed out of Rhode Island) A 4 issue magazine per year subscription listing many Rhode Island genealogies.

Military Records. By James Newell Arnold. 12 volumes. One copy of the set is located at the Mormon Library at Salt Lake City, UT.

The Rhode Island Historical Quarterly. Pub. by Rhode Island Historical Society.

Genealogical Dictionary. By John O. Austin. Reprint of 1887 work. Pub. by Scholarly. If used with G. Andrews Moriarty's additions and corrections, is a very good genealogical source.

The Narragansett Historical Register. Listing many people from the Washington County area. Pub. by Narragansett Historical Society.

Rhode Island Colonial Records. By Joseph Jencks Smith. Vol. 2 is civil and military list, 1647 to 1800. A list of all officers elected by the General Assembly from the organization of the legislative government of the colony to 1800. Vol. 2 covers the revolutionary war period. Pub. by Preston & rounds Co., Providence, RI, 1900.

The Providence Oath of Allegiance and its Signers. Author and publisher unknown. Taken from *Locating Your Revolutionary War Ancestor,* by James C. and Lila Neagles. Pub. by The Everton Pub. Inc., 1983.

Runaways, Deserters, And Notorious Villains From Rhode Island Newspapers, Vol. I: The Providence Gazette, 1762-1800.
By Maureen Alice Taylor. Pub. by Picton Press, 1995.
Lists 1,738 persons which some are Patriot deserters who may have become Loyalists.

MASSACHUSETTS

The Massachusetts State Archives

Columbia Point
220 Morrissey Blvd.
(Dorchester) Boston, MA 02125
Phone: 617-727-2816

The archives has a large reading and research room that can accommodate up to 70 people, and includes public meeting rooms for up to 250 people.

Early records for Maine are housed here. This state was part of Massachusetts until 1820, as mentioned before. The Eastern Lands Collections are the main source for these records, mostly dated from 1783 to 1867. These include deed books too.

Massachusetts Archives card index dated c. 1629 to 1799.

Suffolk County Court files dated 1629-1797 with an index. This is a major collection.

Suffolk County Court House

Boston, MA 02201

Probate, deeds and the old Superior Court of Judicature (since 1785), Supreme Judicial Court of the Commonwealth (indexed).

Middlesex County Court House

208 Cambridge St.
Cambridge, MA 02141

They have pre-1871 probate records on microfilm located on the third floor. Indexes are located on the second floor.

Boston Public Library

Copley Square
Boston, MA 02117

They have all the Massachusetts newspapers on microfilm. Massachusetts town vital records to 1850 (published series)

Various publications of early Boston and state.

W.P.A. index to the genealogical pages of the Boston Transcript.

The Massachusetts Historical Society

1154 Boylston St.
Boston, MA 02215

The Twing Collection for the colonial period, along with other collections which are located on cardex.

The New England Historical Genealogical Society

101 Newbury St.
Boston, MA 02116

This society is one of the oldest and largest genealogical collections in the world, not counting the Mormon collection at Salt Lake City, Utah.

Town vital records. Massachusetts vital records to 1850 (printed series).

The Corbin Manuscript Collection, by Walter E. Corbin. A major collection of church and town gravestone inscriptions that covers 1650 to 1850.

A very large collection of Canadian records. All Canadian census and Maritime Province records, including Ontario and Quebec. They probably have the largest collection on the eastern seaboard next to the Maritimes, adding to it on a monthly basis.

Waldo Chamberlain Sprague, *Genealogies of the Families of Braintree, Massachusetts* dated 1640-1850.

Volumes 1 through 4, plus updated supplements to the "Circulating Collection Catalog" which lists thousands of books, printed matter and collections that are held at the library.

They also have family genealogies, maps, and books on thousands of surnames.

Loyalist House

10 Edgehill Rd.
Haverhill, MA 01830

Owned by Frank J. Bostick Jr. He is the author of several Loyalist works and is a Loyalist genealogist. His works are:

Artie Bostick, Tory. A story about a Loyalist boy growing up in Massachusetts during the American Revolution. This is a very warm story told through the eyes of Artie.

Separate Beachheads. A story about the Bostock/Bostick family as they get involved in several battles in Charlestown and Long Island, and when they finally end up in Nova Scotia.

Bagpipes at the Brandywine. An action filled story about the Loyalists in battle.

State Library Annex

State House
Boston, MA 02133

They carry many city directories.

Loyalist Genealogists

Frank J. Bostick Jr.
Loyalist House
10 Edgehill Rd.
Haverhill, MA 01830

Paul J. Bunnell, FACG,UE
100 Whitehall Rd. #15
Amesbury, MA 01913
E-mail – Benjamin@Amesbury.net
Web Site – http://members.TheGlobe.com/Loyalists/index.htm

Sturgis Library

Rt. 6A
Barnstable, MA 02668

They have the finest genealogical collection located in Southern Massachusetts, pertaining mostly to Cape Cod families.

Genealogical Notes of Cape Cod Families 1620-1901. Compiled by Lydia B. Brownson. This is a hand written record.

Massachusetts Vital Records to 1850 (Has most town in Massachusetts).

Genealogical card file of thousands of names to the library collection.

A very large marine library consisting of hundreds of books.

Cape Cod family genealogies in books and manuscripts.

Cemetery records.

Note: There is a charge for non-Barnstable county residents.

City Registrar's Office

Boston, MA 02201

Boston, Suffolk County vital records.
Birth records ---------------- 1630-1799.
Index of births -------------- 1630-1955.
Marriage records------------ 1646-1890.
Index to marriage records - 1646-1955.
Death records --------------- 1630-1970.
Index to death records ----- 1630-1970.

Note: The above records are also located at the Family History Library, Salt Lake City, Utah 84150.

Other Massachusetts Records

Colony records 1629-1777 (for Massachusetts General Court). Located at the Family History Library, Salt Lake City, UT 84150.

Court Records dated 1664-1781 on index cards, located at the Family History Library, Salt Lake City, UT 84150.

Suffolk County Court of Common Pleas records dated 1701-1855 (indexed) located at the Family History Library, Salt Lake City, UT 84150.

Suffolk County Supreme Judicial Court records dated 1686-1799, also located at the Family History Library, Salt Lake City, UT 84150.

Tax records and property valuations dated c. 1760-1811, located at the Family History Library, Salt Lake City, UT 84150.

Massachusetts, Secretary of the Commonwealth. *Massachusetts Soldiers and Sailors of the Revolutionary War.* 17 volumes. By Wright & Potter Printing Co., State Printers, Boston, 1896 (At the Boston Public Library, Boston, MA 02108, and other locations throughout Massachusetts. (Please keep in mind that this collection is for Patriots, but many changed sides and you could find your Loyalist listed here).

Massachusetts Books and Materials

Divided Hearts, Massachusetts Loyalists 1765-1790. A Biographical Directory compiled by David E. Maas. Pub. by The Society of Colonial Wars in The Commonwealth of Massachusetts and The New England Historical Genealogical Society, 1980.

A Research Guide to the Massachusetts Courts and Their Records. By Catherine S. Menand. Mass. Supreme Judicial Court Archives and Records Preservation. Pub. by Supreme Judicial Court Archives and Record Preservation (Congregation), 1987.

An Inventory of the Records of the Particular Churches of Massachusetts Gathered 1620-1805. By Harold Field Worthley. Harvard University Press, Cambridge, MA, 1970.

The Loyalists of Massachusetts. By Edward Alfred Jones. Reprinted by Genealogical Pub. Co., Baltimore, MD, 1930.

The Loyalists of Massachusetts and the Other Side of the American Revolution. By James Henry Stark, 1910. Reprinted by Kelley Co.

Genealogical Research in Massachusetts, A Guide. By The NEHGS Register, reprinted by Ralph J. Crandall.

The Essex Antiquarian. 13 volumes. Pub. by The Essex Society of Genealogists. (One set can be found at The Amesbury Library, Amesbury, MA 01913.

The Essex Genealogist. A newsletter by Essex Society of Genealogists, Lynnfield, MA 01940.

Essex Institute Historical Collection. By The Essex Institute, 132-134 Essex St., Salem, MA 01970 (Indexed).

The Genealogical Advertiser. Reprint. 4 volumes. Pub. by The Genealogical Pub. Co., 1974, Author, Lucy H. Greenlaw.

MASSOG, newsletter of the Massachusetts Society of Genealogists.

The New England Historical Genealogical Society Register, by NEHGS, 101 Newbury St., Boston, MA 02116. Over 110 volumes mostly indexed. (Heritage Books Inc., Bowie, MD. Is presently republishing the entire set.

Early Massachusetts Marriages Prior to 1800. By Frederic Bailey. Pub. by Genealogical Pub. Co., 1968. Reprint from 1897 work.

Index of Obituaries in Boston Newspapers, 1704-1800. By G.K. Hall. 3 volumes. Pub. by Boston Athenaeum, 1967.

Boston Marriages from 1700-1809. By Edward W. McGlenen. 2 volumes. Pub. by Genealogical Pub. Co., Baltimore, MD, 1977. A reprint of 1898 & 1903. Pub. by Boston Registry Dept. (vols 28, 30).

Massachusetts Soldiers and Sailors of the Revolutionary War. 17 volumes. By Mass. Dept. of Secretary of State. (You may find loyalists that changed sides in this Patriot set).

Massachusetts Officers and Sailors in the French and Indian Wars 1755-1756. Edited by K. David Goss and David Zarowin.

The Massachusetts Tax Valuation List of 1771. By Bette Hobbs Pruitt.

Publications of the Colonial Society of Massachusetts (63 volumes). Pub. by The Boston Colonial Society of Mass.).

Essex County, Massachusetts Probate Index 1638-1840. 2 volumes. By Melinda Lutz Sanborn.

The Town Officials of Colonial Boston 1634-1775. By Robert Francis Seybolt.

The Massachusetts Civil List for the Colonial and Provincial Periods 1630-1774. By William H. Whitmore. Pub. by The Genealogical Pub. Co., MD.

New England Genealogical Research, A Guide to Sources. Compiled by Kip Sperry. Pub. by Heritage Books Inc., 1988.

Massachusetts Periodicals and Newsletters

The American Genealogist. By Ruth Wilder Sherman (and possibly other authors). Was a quarterly magazine with New England genealogies. (Found at many larger libraries).

The Essex Genealogist. Essex Society of Genealogists, Lynnfield Public Library, 18 Summer St., Lynnfield, MA 01940.

(Many others listed throughout the Massachusetts section)

NEW HAMPSHIRE

Note: Please take note that many Loyalists, under cover, came back into the United States after the terrible winter of 1783. Many records in northern states like New Hampshire and Vermont may contain your Loyalist ancestor.

State of New Hampshire

Bureau of Vital Records & Statistics
Health and Welfare Building
Hazen Drive
Concord, NH 03301
Phone: 603-271-4651

Birth records - (some) 1640-1901
Marriages ----- (some) 1640-1938
Deaths --------- (some) 1640-1938
Divorces ------ 1808-1938

New Hampshire State Library

20 Park St.
Concord, NH 03301

This library contains very little Revolutionary War records, but does have:

D.A.R. Lineage Books.

Historical Register of Officers of the Continental Army. By Francis Heitman.

Rolls of the Soldiers in the Revolutionary War. By Isaac Hammond.

Note: These records may show your Loyalist ancestor before they changed sides during the war.

New Hampshire Historical Society

30 Park St.
Concord, NH 03301

They have many works on Patriot soldiers, but pertaining to their pensions, which would not make these men Loyalists. They do have the following:

Deaths of Revolutionary Soldiers. Compiled from Early New Hampshire Newspapers, by Marion Driscoll.

History of the First New Hampshire Regiment. By Frederic Kidder.

New Hampshire State Archives

Records & Archives
71 S. Fruit St.
Concord, NH 03301

This archives has the best holdings for the Revolutionary War period for this state.

Provincial and State Papers of New Hampshire.

Returns of the Association Test 1776.

Treasurers Accounts, War of the Revolution 1775-1783.

Account Book, Revolution 1775-1783.

Account Book of the First and Second Regiments 1780.

Account Book of Various Military Officers 1780.

Revolutionary War Rolls (11 volumes).

Army Rolls 1774-1793 (3 volumes).

Pay Rolls of Militia 1775-1784 (11 volumes).

Joseph Cilley's Regimental Book 1776.

Col. James Reid's Regimental Book, Second New Hampshire Regiment.

Capt. Isaac Farwell's Company Book 1777-1782.

Capt. Ebenezer Fry's Company Book 1781.

Note: Please keep in mind, these are Patriot Rolls, but could contain deserters to the Loyalist cause).

Family History Library

(Mormon Library)
Salt Lake City, UT 84150
Phone: 801-240-2331

This library contains the following information on every state, including New Hampshire as the following:

Provincial Census 1767 & 1775.

Miscellaneous Province and State Papers c. 1641-1800.

New Hampshire Pension Records 1776-1850 (Copied by Mrs. Amos G. Draper).

Piscataqua Pioneers. (Application for membership, lineage papers and personal histories).

Deeds & Probate records 1623-1772 (indexed).

Revolutionary and other military war rolls (indexed).

Revolutionary War Rolls 1775-1783.

Tax Books, 1727-1788 (inventories of Polls and Estates).

Also, at the Family History Library:

Historical New Hampshire. Pub. by New Hampshire Historical Society, Concord, NH. Local histories and articles.

New Hampshire Societies

New Hampshire Society of Genealogist:

Rockingham County Chapter
P.O. Box 81
Exeter, NH 03801

Keene NH Chapter
Keene, NH 03431

New Hampshire Books & Materials

The New Hampshire Genealogical Record. 7 volumes. By Charles W. Tibbetts.
Vital Records, Church & Genealogies. By Genealogical & Historical Society, Dover, NH, July 1903 to April 1910. An illustrated Quarterly Magazine devoted to genealogical biography. Reprinted by Genealogical Reprints, West Jordan, UT, 1983, & Heritage Books, Bowie, MD, 1988.

Genealogical Dictionary of Maine and New Hampshire. By Charles Thornton Libby & Sybil Noyes & Walter Goodwin Davis. Pub. by Southworth Press, Portland, ME, 1928. Reprint by Genealogical Pub., Baltimore, MD, 1988. Reference sources for both states listing families and genealogies.

New Hampshire's Role in the American Revolution, 1763-1789. By The New Hampshire American Revolution Bicentennial Commission. A bibliography of historical and Revolutionary War titles. Published in New London, NH, 1974. Can be ordered through the New Hampshire State Library.

New Hampshire As A Royal Province. By William Henry Fry. Pub. by AMS Press, 1970.

New Hampshire Genealogical Research Guide. By Laird C. Towle & Ann N. Bromn. Pub. by Heritage Books, Inc., Bowie, MD, 1983.

Tories of New Hampshire in the War of the Revolution. By Otis Grant Hammond. Pub. by Gregg Press, Boston, MA, 1972. Reprinted from New Hampshire Historical Society, Concord, NH. Edition, 1917. A study of Loyalists in New Hampshire, about 200 men.

VERMONT

Vermont is another Canadian border state that saw a lot of Loyalists sneak back down after the harsh winter of 1783, and later on, so many Vermont families could have Loyalist blood. Keep in mind that New York and New Hampshire disputed control of this state, and it was once called the New Hampshire Grants by New Hampshire, and the New York Territory by New York.

There were a few battles fought over Vermont. Out of this struggle came the Green Mountain Boys who fought in the Revolutionary War very hard on the side of the Patriots. Led by Ethan Allen, they later met up with Benedict Arnold, and engaged in a battle at Fort Ticonderoga and other northern campaigns. For a short time, this state declared itself the state of New Connecticut, but six months later changed it to Vermont. Also keep in mind that there was the Battle of Bennington which caused many soldiers to desert to the Loyalist side, so these records are very important too.

State of Vermont

Agency of Administration
Vital Records
Public Records Division
6 Baldwin St.
Montpelier, VT 05602
Phone: 802-828-3286

Births, Marriages and Deaths – 1764-1954 (indexed)

Vermont State Library

111 State St.
Supreme Court Building
Montpelier, VT 05602

This library is limited in genealogical and military records, but does have the following:

Vermont Legislature. *Rolls of Soldiers in the Revolutionary War 1775-1783*, by John E. Goodrich. Pub. by Tuttle Co., Rutland, VT, 1904.

Office of Vermont Public Records

6 Baldwin St.
Montpelier, VT 05602

Located just a short distance from the state library, this office contains only:

Rolls of Soldiers in the Revolutionary War, by John E. Goodrich.

Service Records for Vermont Troops, on microfilm roll number 90

Other Vermont Records

Each town has records starting as far back as 1770 to 1870.

14 volumes of military records are located at the Family History Library, Salt Lake City, UT.

Each town has land records.

Vermont Societies

The Genealogical Society of Vermont
46 Chestnut St.
Brattleboro, VT 05301-3152

They produce a newsletter called *Branches & Twigs*, which contains vital records and Vermont genealogies.

Vermont Historical Society
109 State St.
Montpelier, VT 05602

They have the following records:

D.A.R. Patriot Index.
Some of the Earliest Oaths of Allegiance to the United States, by Nellie Waldenmaier.

With Ethan Allen at Ticonderoga, May 10, 1775, by Robert Bascom.

There is a very large collection at this location, including material from the Vermont Society of Colonial Dames, which could be of some help.

Vermont Books & Materials

Vermont Historical Gazetteer. Quarterly magazine by Abby M. Hemenway, printed long ago.

A Guide to Vermont's Repositories. By Vermont State Archives 1986.

Collecting Vermont Ancestors. By Alice Eichholz, 1986. Guidebook to major genealogical sources in Vermont.

The Vermont Antiquarian. 3 volumes of vital records, church and grave records. Pub. by Research Pub. Co., Burlington, VT, 1902-5.

The Vermonter. By Charles R. Cummings, White River Junction, VT. Historical articles of interest. Newsletter.

The 1798 Census in Vermont, by Betty Bandel in The New England Historical and Genealogical Register #137, Jan. 1983, pages 4-17. Pub. by NEHGS.

Collections of the Vermont Historical Society. 10 volumes. Pub. by the society. New York land grants in Vermont and historical material.

Vermont 1771 Census. By Jay Mack Holbrook. Pub. by Holbrook Research Institute 1982. Not quite a census, but lists early settlers of the area.

Vermont Confiscation's and Sale of Estates.
Copied by Lt. Col. H.C. Burleigh MD, CM, UE.
Copies at UEL, Toronto, Canada.

NEW YORK

Southern New York fell to the British right at the beginning of the war and was controlled throughout the revolution, especially New York City, which became the center for refugees coming in from all over the colonies. After Benedict Arnold changed sides in 1780, he was credited with creating the American Loyalists regiments including The American Legion Regiment. By using this untapped resource that the British thought had no value, this author feels that this organization of Loyalist refugees gave birth to the United Empire Loyalists during the occupation of New York City in 1781.

The "Great Exodus of 1783" began here, and nearly forty thousands refugees fled New York City for Nova Scotia on several fleets, starting in May 1783. Most of the governing forces for British North America came from New York City.

New York State Archives

11 D40 Cultural Education Center
Empire State Plaza
Albany, NY 12230
Phone: 518-474-1195
Website: http://unix6.nysed.gov.gopher://unix6.nysed.gov:70/11/

A fire in 1911 destroyed many records, but you can find:

Muster Rolls, and lists of soldiers.

State Auditor Records (and others). Called Accession #93, vol. A & B, they are the main section for Revolutionary War records. Also, Accession #253 which refers to the soldiers.

New York State Census – 1776 & 1782.

New York State Library

Cultural Educational Center
Empire State Plaza
Albany, NY 12223
Website: http://unix2.nysed.gov/gengen.htm

This library has a history and genealogy section and many works on the Revolutionary War period.

Couples who had bonds posted for marriage will appear in The New York Marriages Previous to 1784 (H974.7, N548, 1968), but many of these bonds were destroyed in the fire of 1911. Abstracts can be found in The New York Marriage Bonds 1753-1783 (H974.7, S427N), but the original bonds are in the custody of the New York State Archives in Albany.

New York Historical Society

170 Central Park West
New York City, NY 10024
Phone: 212-873-3400

There is a very large collection of Revolutionary War documents available. A card index is located at the front counter of the library. The library carries material on the history of the state and nearby areas, maps, manuscripts and newspapers. There is a small admission fee.

Orderly books.

Revolutionary War muster and pay rolls dated 1775-83.

610 original papers on inventories of estates located in the southern district of New York.

Church records of nearly all New York City except the German Reformed church.

The Haviland Records Room

15 Rutherford Place
New York City, NY 10003

The largest Quaker collection outside of Swarthmore College, Pennsylvania. (Many Quakers were caught up in the struggle and were banished or disowned).

The New York Yearly Meeting at one time claimed over 20,000 members; therefore, this library is very important, but challenging to the researcher because the Friends (Quakers) did not keep the genealogist in mind when they recorded their monthly and yearly meetings. They can be very hard to read.

These records lists births, deaths, marriages, minutes of meetings and removals. The latter would be of interest to Loyalist hunters because if the Quakers took part in the Revolution they were disowned and removed from the books. But that does not mean they were completely forgotten because their Meeting House supplied the needy Loyalists in Canada with food, clothing and supplies after 1783, and recorded them in their books, including names of the refugees they helped.

Volume 111 of William Wade Hinshaw's *Encyclopedia of American Quaker Genealogy* indexes names of members from New York City and Long Island Friends Meetings.

This Reading Room also carries records for Hardwick, Mendham, Shrewsbury, Rahway, Plainfield, and other New Jersey Meeting Houses; Amawalk, Chappaqua and Purchase Monthly Meetings in Westchester County, New York; Creek, Nine Partners, Oblong, Oswego and Stanford Monthly Meetings in Dutchess County, New York; Chatham and Hudson Monthly Meetings in Columbia County, New York; and Rochcester Monthly Meeting in Monroe County, New York. There are also abstracts for Westchester, Ulster, Columbia, Albany, Clinton, Niagara and Ontario Counties.

New York City Public Library

5th Avenue at 42nd St.
New York City, NY 10018
Local History & Genealogy Room 315G
Phone: 212-930-0828

They have an entire room devoted to history and genealogy. There are 215 publications on the Revolution which this library says is the largest collection on the East Coast next to the Library of Congress in Washington, D.C.

Some excellent samples of Loyalist books that you will find at this library are:

The Loyalist Press in the American Revolution 1765-1781, By Timothy M. Barnes (ZMB-892)

The Loyalist, A Historical Novel. By Jane West (1758-1852). Ford Collection.

New Jersey Gazette. Burlington 1777 to Dec. 5, 1778 (Rare Book Div.) Newspaper.

Monmouth Democrat. Freehold, NJ Newspaper. Weekly mounted clippings of Monmouth County, NJ Newspaper.

Loyalist Operations at New Haven, Connecticut. By William L. Clements, Michigan University and K.P. Timothy.

New Jersey Gazette. 1778 March 4 to Dec. 31, 1779, Jan. 6 to May 12, Dec. 29, 1780 Jan. 5 – April 12, 27 June 14, 1781 Jan. 3 – 1783 July 16, 1786 Jan. 2. (Rare Book Div.) Weekly Newspapers.

The New York Genealogical and Biographical Society

122 East 58th St.
New York City, NY 10022-1939
Phone: 212-755-8532

Reformed Dutch Church records and nearly all other New York City churches are located here. A very important source. This society specializes in New York and Northeast genealogy. Manuscripts and microfilm available to members. They take a minimum donation for daily visitors who are not members.

This fine society has over 63,000 volumes of genealogies, 23,000 manuscripts, 3,000 microfilms.

Land Records

Land papers, Council Minutes and Patents at Albany State Library.

New York Books & Materials

Records of the Revolutionary War. By William Saffell.

New York Archives. *New York in the Revolution.* By Berthold Fernow.

Comptroller's Office. *New York in the Revolution as Colony and State.*

Joseph Brant, 1743-1807: Man of Two Worlds. By Isabel T. Kelsay. Pub. by Syracuse University Press, 1984. A Mohawk Loyalist from New York.

Genealogical Data from Colonial New York Newspapers. Compiled by Kenneth Scott. Pub. by Genealogical Pub. Co., 1982. Material taken from the New York Gazette, New York Mercury and New York Gazette and Weekly Mercury.

Calendar of Wills on File and Recorded in the Office of the Clerk of the Court of Appeals of the County Clerk at Albany and of the State of New York 1626-1836. By The Colonial Dames of the State of New York, 1896.

Greener Pastures: The Loyalist Experience of Benjamin Ingraham.
By Earle Thomas. Pub. by Mika Pub., Ontario, 1983.
Story about a New York Loyalist who flees to New Brunswick, Canada.

Confiscation's Lists of Albany, Charlotte & Tryon Counties, New York.
Housed at the State Library, Albany, NY.

The New York Gazette and Weekly Mercury Newspapers.
Years: 1780-83. Can be requested on interlibrary loan.

Loyalism in New York during the American Revolution.
By A.C. Flick. Pub. by Arno Press, 1969/70

War Out of Niagara.
By H. Swiggett. Pub. by Columbia University Press, 1933.

Disposition of Loyalist Estates in the Southern District of the State of New York.
By H.B. Yoshpe. Pub by Columbia University Press, 1939.

The Confiscation and Sale of the Loyalist Estates and Its Effect Upon the Democratization of Landholding in New York State, 1799-1800.
By John Thomas Reily, 1974

De Lancey's Brigade (Loyalist) 1776-1778 Orderly Book of the Three Battalions of Loyalists, Commanded by Brigadier-General Oliver De Lancey, 1776-1778 New York.
Printed by New York Historical Society, 1917.

Orderly Book of Sir John Johnson During the Oriskany Campaign, 1776-1777, Albany, New York.
Published by Joel Munsell's Sons, 1882.

Comptroller's Office. New York in the Revolution as Colony and State, Supplement. Albany, New York.
By New York State. Published by J.B. Lyon Co., 1901

Commission for Detecting and Defeating Conspiracies, 1777-1778. Minutes of the Commissioners for Detecting and Defeating Conspiracies in the State of New York. Albany County Sessions, 1778-1781.
By The New York State, Albany, NY, 1909.

The Civil Sword: James Delancey's Westchester Refugees, 1776-1785.
By G.R. Vincent. Pub. by Cobequid Press, 1997.

The Liberty We Seek: Loyalist Ideology in Colonial New York & Massachusetts.
By Janice Potter, Cambridge, MA, 1983.

Newspaper

The New York Mercury and *Gazette* dated 1775 to 1783. This is an excellent source of information on the occupation of New York by the British, mostly printing British and American Loyalist happenings. The 1783 issues name the ships that sailed for Nova Scotia during the exodus plus some Loyalist troop lists.

New York Loyalist Internet Locations & Materials

British Headquarters Papers, New York City,
1774-1783, *The Carleton Papers*
By Ed Kipp.
http://www.magma.ca/~ekipp/kingname.htm

New York GenWeb Project
New York Genealogy.
http://www.rootsweb.com/~nygenweb/

Clerk of Surrogate's Court

31 Chambers (Room 301)
New York City, NY 10007
Phone: 212-374-8233)

They will perform a search for a fee. They have probate and estate records containing wills dated from 1665 to 1927. Administration Bonds, 1742-1828. Letters of Administration, 1743-1927 (Many are located at the New York Historical Society on 77th St. & Central Park West, NY, NY).

New York Branch Genealogical Library

Albany State Library
Empire State Library
Albany, NY 02223

Mormon Visitor Center

2 Lincoln Square
New York City, NY 10023
Phone: 212-799-2660

This library is a branch of the main Mormon library in Salt Lake City, Utah. Patrons can request information from many sources (Including Canada) that are located there, including Loyalist material from all locations mentioned in this book.

National Archives – New York Branch (Regional)

Building 22 Military Ocean Terminal
Bayonne, NJ 07002
Phone: 201-823-7252

As mentioned under the National Archives section in this book, the researcher can request all records pertaining to the Revolutionary War period for this area.

Brooklyn Historical Society

128 Pierrepont St.
Brooklyn, NY 11201
Phone: 718-624-0890

Has books, manuscripts, genealogy, local histories, newspapers, photos and vital records. A small fee for non-members.

Queens Borough Public Library

89-11 Merrick Blvd.
Jamaica, NY 11432
Phone: 718-990-0770

Carries Queens and Long Island history and genealogies, maps.

White Plains Public Library

100 Martine Ave.
White Plains, NY 10601
Phone: 914-682-4400

This library has some genealogies and books of history for Westchester County.

History of Rye. By C.W. Baird. This includes Harrison and White Plains till 1788.

New York Genealogical Book Dealers

Argosy Bookstore
166 East 59th St.
New York City, NY 10022

The Hawkins Association Newsletter

P.O. Box 2392
Setauket, Long Island,
NY 11733

This is a family association that is researching their Patriot and Loyalist lines. The newsletter appears to be very informative.

DELAWARE

Public Archives of Delaware

Division of Historical & Cultural Affairs
Bureau of Archives & Records Management
Hall of Records
Dover, DE 19901
Phone: 302-739-5318

The following is what is housed at the archives and at local levels:

Church Records – Holy Trinity Church.

LDS Library Collection – Private collection of vital records.

Military Records – Printed material collected by Leon DeValinger. Revolutionary War in three volumes at Delaware Archives.

Deeds – Located at county level and usually only by an attorney.

Calendar of Wills dated 1682 – 1800 (on microfilm).

Many other vital records written by Leon DeValinger. Carries most state records from earliest time to 1850.

Proprietary Warrants and Surveys dated 1682 – 1776.

Probate and Wills are housed here at the archives. Calendar of Wills contains Kent County for 1680-1800. Others held at court houses in each county.

Delaware Societies and Libraries

University of Delaware
Hugh M. Morris Library
Newark, DE 19716
Phone: 302-831-2000
Website: http://www.lib.udel.edu/ud/spec/exhibits/wartime.html
Library: http://www.lib.edel.edu/

Peninsula Conference Historical Society
Wilmington, DE 19807

The Historical Society of Delaware
6th & Market Streets
Wilmington, DE 19801

The Wilmington Institute Free Library
Wilmington, DE 19807

The News-Journal Company
(For newspapers)
Wilmington, DE 19807

The Memorial Library
University of Delaware at Newark
Newark, DE 19713

Delaware Genealogical Society
505 Market St. Mall
Wilmington, DE 19801

Delaware Swedish Colonial Society
c/o M. Draper (as of 1991)
4830 Kennett Pike
Wilmington, DE 19807

Delaware Loyalist Books & Materials

The Delaware Loyalists. By Harold Bell Hancock. Pub. by Gregg Press, Boston, MA, 1972.

MARYLAND

Note: Many Maryland Loyalists settled around the Fredericton, New Brunswick, Canada area between 1783-1786, which today is a district called Maryland.

Maryland State Archives

Hall of Records
350 Rowe Blvd.
Annapolis, MD 21401
Phone: 410-974-3914 or 410-974-3916
Fax #: 410-974-3895
E-mail: archives@mdarchives.state.md.us
Website: http:/www.mdarchives.state.md.us

The following records are housed in these archives:

Index to Chancery Depositions 1668-1789 (22 Volumes).

Maryland Gleanings in England (Volumes 1-5).

The Maryland Historical and Genealogical Bulletin. By Robert F. Hayes Jr. Contains bible, militia, county and marriage records.

Baltimore City's Dead Prior to 1806. Has gravestone inscriptions.

The Archives of Maryland. Pub. by Maryland Historical Society, Baltimore, MD, 1883-1972. (72 Volumes).

Proceedings and Acts of Assembly 1637-1774. (32 Volumes) Pub. by The Maryland Historical Society, 1883-?

Journals and Correspondence of the Council of Safety 1775-1777 and the State Council 1777-1784. (8 Volumes) Pub. by The Maryland Historical Society, 1897. Printed by the State.

Probate prior to 1777 were at county courts, but also at Central Prerogative Court, which is preserved.

Wills, inventories and estates are here at the archives even though the county court house was destroyed by fire. The Hall of Records has all the original Wills and other estate papers. (Maryland colonial inventories are unique because they list the two nearest relatives and two of the greatest creditors. There are 7 volumes dated 1751-1777 containing balances of Final Distribution of Estates. Wills are on microfilm.

Births and Deaths (early) on cardex. 1804-1877.

Marriages (From about 1777 - mid-1800).

Marriage and Death notices from Maryland Gazette dated 1727-34, 1745-1821 in volumes 17,18,42 of Maryland Historical Magazine.

Census of 1776 and 1778 to determine free white males over 18 years who had failed to take the oath of allegiance. Found on cardex.

Military muster and pay rolls for 1732-72 on cardex.

Revolutionary records in Archives of Maryland, vol. 18. Others found on cardex.

Calendar of Maryland State Papers, covers *The Black Books* (Proprietary and Royal Papers 1636-1785), *The Bank Stock Papers* (Maryland stock in the Bank of England), *The Brown Books* (Government and military communications 1747-1803), *The Red Books* (3 Volumes, state papers 1773-1825), *The Executive Miscellanea (1684-1821)*. Two thirds of the *Calendar of Maryland State Papers* deals with 1775-1778.

Maryland Societies & Libraries

Maryland Historical Society
201 West Monument St.
Baltimore, MD 21201
Phone: 301-685-3750

Maryland State Law Library
361 Rowe Blvd.
Annapolis, MD 21401
Phone: 301-974-3395

Enoch Pratt Free Library
400 Cathedral St.
Baltimore, MD 21201
Phone: 301-396-5468

Peabody Library
17 East Mount Vernon Place
Baltimore, MD 21202
Phone: 301-659-8197

Maryland Genealogical Society
201 West Monument St.
Baltimore, MD 21201

Note: There are other societies located in each county, but too many to mention. You can get a list from one of the above societies for the area you are interested in.

Maryland Books & Materials

There is much written about Maryland, and new material comes out nearly every year.

The Colonial Period of American History. By Charles McLean Andrews. Pub. by Yale University Press. 4 Vols., 1975.

History of Maryland From the Earliest Period to the Present Day. Vol. 3. By John T. Scharf. Pub. by Gale, 1967. Reprint of 1879 work.

The Lords Baltimore and the Maryland Palatinate. By Clayton C. Hall. Pub. by Nunn & Co., Baltimore, MD, 1904. Six Lectures on Maryland Colonial History delivered before the Johns Hopkins University 1902. Also available in microfiche.

Maryland Historical Magazine. Vols 1-65. By Maryland Historical Society. On microfilm by University of Ann Arbor Michigan, Ann Arbor, Michigan 1906.

Maryland Historical and Genealogical Bulletin. 21 Volumes. Pub. by Maryland Historical and Genealogical Society. July 1930 to Oct. 1950.

Maryland Colonial Wills 1634-1777. 8 Volumes. By James M. Magruder. Pub. by Genealogical Pub. Co., Baltimore, MD. Reprinted from 1933 edition at Annapolis, MD.

Maryland Colonial Abstracts. 5 Volumes. By James M. Magruder. Pub. by Genealogical Pub. 1968. Reprint from 1934-39 edition (self published) in Annapolis, MD.

The Maryland-Delaware Genealogist. By Raymond B. Clark Jr. No date and no author listed. To inquire, contact the Maryland Genealogical Society in Annapolis, MD.

An Inventory of Maryland State Papers, The Era of the American Revolution 1775-1789. (can be bought at the state archives). Published by the Maryland State Archives.

Robert Alexander, Maryland Loyalist. A biography of this leading loyalist from Maryland. By Janet Bassett Johnson. Pub. by Gregg Press, Boston, MA, 1972.

Maryland Book Publishers Dealing With Loyalist Materials

Heritage Books, Inc.
1540E Pointer Ridge Place
Bowie, MD 20716

Genealogical Publishing Co., Inc.
Baltimore, MD 21233

NEW JERSEY

New Jersey was one of the hot spots during the American Revolution. The colony was split three ways over separation: for, against, and the rest trying to stay neutral. Many large important battles were fought here. George Washington spent much of his time encamped throughout the countryside of New Jersey. Like records of other areas, New Jersey's Loyalist documentation was scattered or destroyed because of widespread destruction and the movement from one area to another. Keep in mind, nearly all Loyalists became Refugees. These factors will make your search that much harder.

The following sources are what this state has to offer. Tax lists substituted for early colony census because many were destroyed. The New Jersey records have much to offer because of all the hard-working and dedicated genealogists who live there.

The New Jersey State Library & Archives

Bureau of Archives & Records Preservation
CN-307, 185 W. State St.
Trenton, NJ 08625
Phone: 609-292-6294 or 609-292-6274

New Jersey documents share the first floor with the law department; The Jerseyana and Genealogy departments occupy the B-level reading room. The Jerseyana material contains New Jersey history, culture, geography, politics, etc.

The genealogical material contains county and local histories, genealogical guidebooks, published genealogies, passenger lists and census records. This collection also includes other state materials. Because of the migration patterns of the New Jersey population, many families in this area traveled back and forth throughout all the surroundings colonies. There are several hundred maps going back to the seventeenth century to the present day. You must keep in mind that many families from New Jersey traveled many times to New York, more than to any other colony.

Many Loyalist records can be found in the court system of New Jersey. The following are those courts listed in order by degree of their final judgement:

Justice of the Peace: Small claims. Records not on microfilm.

District Court: Minor cases. Records not on microfilm.

Court of Common Pleas: Marriages, naturalizations, child support, old age assistance. A few are on microfilm.

Orphan's Court: Estates and guardianships. Many on microfilm.

Circuit Court of the State Supreme Court: Marriages, mortgage foreclosures, estate partitions, debts, wrongful acts. Records not on microfilm.

Court of Quarter Sessions: Desertions, apprenticeships, disputes, vice. Records on microfilm.

Court of Oyer and Teriner: Criminal cases such as treason and murder. Not on microfilm.

Court of Chancery: Mortgage foreclosures, protection of women's estate, legacies in trust, watercourse disputes. Some on microfilm.

Prerogative Court: Estate disputes. Most on microfilm.

Supreme Court: Estate disputes, treason, murder, naturalization, appeals. Indexed only. Originals at State Archives.

Keep in mind that when looking for your Loyalist records, you are looking for estates that were probably taken away or sold off throughout the war, and a little after. Treason charges or maybe even murder, desertion or counterfeiting charges, debts not paid, orphans left to the courts and various other criminal acts against the state between the years of 1774-1783, but don't forget the many judgements that were also carried out after the war. It is probably safe to check records going all the way to 1790. Look real closely, because some relatives left behind could have successfully sold property for their Loyalist, child, brother, sister or cousin.

There is a family-name index with significant material on genealogies, histories and biographies. It does not include all New Jersey families, but could prove very helpful to the surname you are trying to find. In the past, the state library staff was very helpful in conducting a limited search, but due to state cutbacks in 1989 by the governor, their time is now spent on other duties. It is always best to inquire before your trip to assure hours and availability.

Because of the large Dutch population you may need to check the Holland Society Collections (surnames A through K, numbers 1,002,769 and from L through Z, numbers 1,002,770). These records consist of forty-seven rolls of microfilm, but are in alphabetical order. Many Dutch families also moved back and forth to New York, so you best check the records of the Holland Society of New York, too.

The earliest regular newspapers in New Jersey start at 1778, so it may be worth your while to check the New York, Philadelphia or even the Boston newspapers before that date for New Jersey information. Extracts from New Jersey newspapers can be found in volumes 1-5 in book form (they are called *New Jersey Archives Newspapers Extracts*). These five volumes cover the Revolutionary War period. The larger set, covering more years can also be found on CD.

Probate records are located at each county level, but the periods from 1665-1804 are here at the library/archives on microfilm. Copies of these records and wills can be requested from the library. Wills dated 1665-1817 have been abstracted and indexed. The first series are volumes 23, 30, 32-42. All microfilmed.

Land records after 1780's should be requested from each county clerk in their respective counties. All deeds before 1780 are here at the library/archives. Also, the index of deeds of grantor and grantee dated 1670 to c.1800 are located here. Many deeds and mortgages were not recorded, so it is suggested that you search road permits or petitions because they list the owners of the land and neighbors' property that the roads run through.

Other microfilm land records are:

East Jersey surveys and indexes, 1678-1814 (film #947,881).

West Jersey surveys and indexes, 1654- 1952 (film #888,803).

West Jersey Warrants, 1600's to 1800's. Many indexed (film #888,815).

Minutes of the Council of Proprietors, West Jersey, 1688-1951 (microfilmed).

Index of Powers of Attorney, Surveyors Reports, Commissions, etc., 1703-1856 (film #542,530 A-I and #542,531 J-Z).

Loyalist Records

Loyalist inquisitions. Listing their land for sale and judgements passed on them.

Military Records

Colonial war records can be of some help because they range from 1665-1774. This means that your Loyalist could have served near the later dates (Microfilm #573,334, items 1 and 3).

Revolutionary war records on microfilm are manuscripts, citations, pension claims, list of Loyalist officers and men of New Jersey and records of damage in New Jersey, 1776-82.

Official Register of the Officers and Men of New Jersey in the Revolutionary War. By William S. Stryker (1872). Reprinted by Genealogical Pub. Co. (on microfilm #908,526).

Death Records

Woodbridge – 1671-1776

Marriage Records

25% of marriages were recorded between 1665-1800 and are located at the archives (Vol. 22 microfilm #874,375). These were filed with the Secretary of the province. Others can be found at each church record, if they survived.

Newspapers

Directory of New Jersey Newspapers, 1765-1970. By William C. Wright and Paul A. Stellhorn (1977). This work lists all newspapers concerning New Jersey and tells you who has a copy for interlibrary loan.

An index to *Vital Statistics in Trenton Newspapers.* Covers death and marriage notices for 1776-1900 (not on microfilm).

The Bureau of Archives and History

(Located in the basement of the New Jersey State Library)
185 W. State St.
Trenton, NJ 08625
Phone: 609-292-6260

Both library and archives compliment each other by being in the same building. The following records may be of use to the Loyalist researcher:

Colonial and state judiciary records, legislative minutes and enrolled laws.

Military records from the colonial period.

War-damage claims filed by British and Americans in New Jersey, 1776-1782; deeds, 1664-1800; wills and inventories, 1681-1900; and tax ratable lists, 1773-1822.

Colonial, state, regional and local maps.

Selected eighteenth and nineteenth century county court records.

New Jersey newspapers on microfilm, 1778-1900's.

Published volumes on New Jersey colonial, state, county and local history; general genealogical research guides, bibliographical compilations.

The New Jersey Tercentenary Commission 1664-1964

Microfilm report of Dr. Richard P. McCormick's visit to Great Britain, June to August 1960 to extract New Jersey records out of British depositories. Many are early colonial histories, but this great undertaking found many Loyalist records also. I took out only what may be of value to the Loyalist researcher. These records can be found at the archives.

The Public Record Office, Chancery Lane, London, England contains the greatest quantity of New Jersey material in Great Britain.

Colonial Office Papers: M, C.O. 5/1002 (Reel 2)

Letters to the Secretary of State from Governor William Franklin, 1776-1781 (Franklin was the last colonial governor of New Jersey, Loyalist and son of Benjamin Franklin). Letters to Earl of Dartmouth discussing conditions during the revolution, intelligence and problems comfronting the Loyalists. There are 57 more letters dated 1768-1782.

War Office: General Court Martial: #3, M, W.O. 71/56 New York City, September 15-25, 1780 (ff. 69-135)(Reel 4).

Charges from Lt. Col. Thomas against Lt. Col. Cosmo Gordon relating to behavior during the battle of Springfield, NJ. Contains detailed information on the battle.

Audit Office: M, A.O. 13 Loyalist Claims (*PLEASE NOTE: This report continues through "Sussex Archaeological Society" below)

The report to Dr. Richard P. McCormick, auditor, says the following:

> The documentation of claims by Loyalists and others, for losses suffered or services rendered during the revolution, is vast and confusing. The major source is A.O. 12, and transcripts to this material are in the New York Public Library. Additional memorials, with supporting documents, are to be found in A.O. 13. Evidently the memorials in most instances duplicate those in A.O. 12. In some instances, the only information extant on particular cases is found in A.O. 13. An investigation of A.O. 13 revealed the names of many Loyalists not recorded in E.A. Jones' *The Loyalists of New Jersey* (Newark 1927).
>
> Because of the wealth of information relating to detailed aspects of the Revolution in New Jersey, it seemed desirable to microfilm all of the material in A.O. 13 involving residents of New Jersey. There is a typescript name index to the items in A.O. 13 in the Public Record Office. In most cases, the name of the claimant is followed by the state in which information about an individual may be found.
>
> Additional Loyalist materials can be found in T. 50/1-56 and T. 79/1-151, but time did not permit any exploration of these classes. All of the A.O. 13 materials listed below have been filmed.

Index to Loyalist Claims on Microfilm

A-D Claims A.O. 13/17 (Reel 5).
E-L New Claims A.O. 13/18 (Reel 5 & 6).
L-P New Claims A.O. 13/19 (Reel 6).
Q-W New Claims A.O. 13/20 (Reel 6 & 7).

A-C Temporary Assistance A.O. 13/108 (Reel 7 & 8).
D-K Temporary Assistance A.O. 13/109 (Reel 8 & 9).
L-O Temporary Assistance A.O. 13/110 (Reel 9 & 10).
O-R Temporary Assistance A.O. 13/111 (Reel 10 & 11).
S-W Temporary Assistance A.O. 13/112 (Reel 11 & 12).

H-L Temporary Assistance A.O. 13/61 (Reel 7).
Note: These are Maryland Loyalists, but there are several petitions which come from New Jersey included here.

In addition to the two main series (A.O. 13/17-20 and A.O. 13/108-112) there are two others. These are A.O. 13/90-107, denominated "Various Papers" and A.O. 13/137-140, labeled "Miscellaneous." Both yield numerous New Jersey items.

A.O. 13/90 (Reel 13) - Contains claims of Ozias Annesley, Ellis Barrow of Woodbridge, NJ; Joseph Barton, Stephen Bedell, Daniel Bowen, Capt. John Burnet and Robert Fitzrandolph also of Woodbridge.

A.O. 13/91 (Reel 13) - Claims of Nathan Lewis of Burlington, NJ and Hannah MacLeod of Elizabeth, NJ.

A.O. 13/92 (Reel 13) - Claims of William Pearson of Essex County, NJ, Isaac Plumb of Newark, NJ, Stacy Potts of Trenton, NJ, John Poulison and Dick Brinkeroff of Bergen, NJ, all for services rendered and Broughton Reynolds of Elizabeth, NJ, and Capt. Samuel Rutherford of Trenton, NJ.

A.O. 13/93 (Reel 13) - Claims of Daniel Cope, with many supporting papers and Rev. George Panton of Trenton, NJ.

A.O. 13/96 (Reel 13) - Claims of Jacob Hall of Cumberland, Abraham Haring of Bergen County, NJ, Cornelius Hetfield Jr. of Elizabeth, NJ, Charles Hart of Connecticut Farms, NJ, Margaret Hutchinson of Hanover Township, NJ, William Hutchinson of Gloucester County, NJ, Benezer Murdock Hingston of Freehold, NJ.

A.O. 13/98 (Reel 13) - Claims of Cornelius Garrabrant and Cornelius Sip of Communipaw, NJ, James Gordon of Bernards Township, NJ.

Note: Time did not permit an examination of A.O. 13/99-107.

A.O. 13/137 (Reel 12 & 18) - Contains rough plans for arming the refugees from New Jersey dated 1778.

A.O. 13/139 (Reel 12 & 18) - Claims and other documents relating to William Alexander, Cornelius Vanderhaven, Thomas Blackney, Cortlandt Skinner and Robert Cooke.

Lambeth Palace Library
London, S.E. 1
Great Britain

Contains various New Jersey documentation including the following Loyalist records:

3. F.P. 72 Colonial Letters of Orders:

Rev. John Preston of Perth Amboy, NJ joined the British 26th Regiment in 1777.

Other letters involve: Rev. Abraham Beach, Rev. John Wicksall, Rev. William Ayers, Rev. Uzal Ogden, Rev. William Frazer, Rev. Thomas Chandler, Rev. Roberta Blackwell.

Sussex Archaeological Society
Barbican House
Lewes, Sussex,,
England, Great Britain

The Gage Papers (Reel 15)

Enormous collection on the Gage family, General Thomas Gage who was married to Margaret Kemble, daughter of Peter Kemble of New Brunswick, and Morristown, New Jersey, but later settled New Brunswick, Canada as a Loyalist (1765-1865)

NOTE: THIS IS THE END OF THE REPORT OF RICHARD P. MCCORMICK, AUDITOR (Audit Office: M, A.O. *13 Loyalist Claims*).

New Jersey Newspapers Important for Loyalist Research

These are located at various libraries and holdings throughout the USA. Consult the *Directory of New Jersey Newspapers 1765-1970* by William C. Wright and Paul A. Stellhorn for their locations and availability.

New Jersey Gazette, 1777-1778 & 1778-1786.
New Jersey Journal, 1779 to c.1783.
Morris-town Gazette and *New Jersey Advertiser*, 1784-85?
Brunswick Gazette and *Weekly Monitor*, 1787-89.

New Brunswick Gazette and Weekly Monitor, 1786-87.
Political Intelligencer and New Jersey Advertiser, 1783-85.
New York Gazette and Weekly Mercury, 1776 (Before British occupation).
Morning Herald and Weekly Advertiser, c.1785.
Trenton Mercury and Weekly Advertiser, 1787.
Trenton Weekly Mercury, 1787-88.

New Jersey Periodicals/Newspapers/Books/Materials

The Genealogical Magazine of New Jersey
Published by the Genealogical Society of New Jersey since 1925 to the present. Volumes 1-40 (1925-65) are indexed.

New Jersey History
Published by The New Jersey Historical Society at Newark NJ since 1845 to the present. Volumes 1-36 (1845-1919) have an index.

Morris Area Genealogy Society Newsletter
Published by the society and was an award winning newsletter in 1989.

Gleanings from the West Fields
Published by The Genealogical Society of the West Fields, Westfield, NJ. This is an excellent source for general info. and genealogy.

Revolutionary Census of New Jersey
By Kenn Stryker-Rodda. Published by Hunterdon House. This is a main source for locating Loyalists.

New Jersey Marriages Records, 1665-1800
By William Nelson. Published by Genealogical Pub. Co., MD. A very helpful source for locating your Loyalist marriage records.

Guide to the Manuscripts Collections of New Jersey Historical Society
Compiled by Don C. Skemer & Robert C. Morris. Pub. by The New Jersey Historical Society.

New Jersey Historical Manuscripts
Compiled by Mary R. Murin. Pub. by The New Jersey Historical Commission. A guide to collections in the state.

Notices from New Jersey Newspapers, 1781-1790
By Thomas B. Wilson. Pub. by Hunterdon House, NJ (1988).

Some Early Records of Morris County, New Jersey, 1740-1799
By Harriet Stryker-Rodda

Historical and Genealogical Miscellany (New York and New Jersey)
By John E. Stillwell, M.D. (1906). Miscellaneous records such as Bible records, marriages, births and deaths (Vols. 1-5).

Given Name Index to the Genealogical Magazine of New Jersey
By Kenn Stryker-Rodda. Pub. by Hunterdon House, NJ. This is a three volume set index to the magazine.

New Jersey Archives Newspapers Extracts, Vol. 1-5
Edited by W. Stryker. Pub. by John L. Murphy Pub. Co., 1901-2.

New Jersey Societies and Libraries

The New Jersey Historical Society Library
230 Broadway St.
Newark, NJ 07104

The following collections are located at this society:

New Jersey State Society, Daughters of the America Revolution Library, c. 1,000 volumes of records.

The Genealogical Vertical Files. About 10,000 folders in 19 file drawers.

Elias Boudinot Stockton Genealogical Collection. 75,000 cards, around 1,500 folders including some New York families.

Freeman Worth Gardner Genealogical Collection. About 35,000 cards on families from Woodbridge and vicinity.

Charles Carroll Gardner Genealogical Collection. About 30,000 cards, 29 notebooks, 180 folders and manuscripts (More of this collection is housed at Rutgers University Library in Brunswick, NJ).

New Jersey Tax Ratables, 1778-1832.

Family Bible records. About 400 files.

Family files. About 1,200.

Surname index to family genealogies, including some works on:
Allen Family, A. Van Doren Honeyman, Charles G.B. Conger, Canfield-Dickerson, Gardner, Jouet, J.A. Robertson, Marsh, Mahlon Johnson Family, O.B. Leonard, Phillips, Cook, Shipman, Reed, Winans, Plume, Ross Families.

The Following Libraries and Societies carry historical records of their areas, which will be of help if your Loyalist comes from that county. Many have genealogies too:

Joint Free Public Library of Morristown and Morris Township
1 Miller Rd.
Morristown, NJ 07960

Monmouth County Historical Association
70 Court St.
Freehold, NJ 07728

Atlantic City Public Library
Illinois and Pacific Avenues
Atlantic City, NJ 08401

Burlington County Library
Woodland Rd.
Mt. Holly, NJ 08060

Camden County Historical Society
Euclid Ave. & Park Blvd.
Camden, NJ 08103

Cape May Historical Society
Courthouse
Cape May, NJ 08204

Glassboro State College
Glassboro, NJ 08028

Gloucester County Historical Society Library
17 Hunter St.
Woodbury, NJ 08096

Hunterdon County Historical Society
Hiram E. Deats Memorial Library
114 Main St.
Flemington, NJ 08822

Neptune Township Historical Society
25 Neptune Blvd.
Neptune, NJ 07753

North Jersey Highlands Historical
MS Vi Hill
177 Valley Rd.
Wayne, NJ 07470

Passaic County Historical Society
The Lambert Castle
Garrett Mt. Reservation
Paterson, NJ 07509

Princton University Library
The Princton, NJ 08540

Salem County New Jersey Historical Society
81-83 Market St.
Salem, NJ 08079

Vineland Historical and Antiquarian Society
108 So. Seventh St.
Vineland, NJ 10028

Westfield Memorial Library
425 East Broad St.
Westfield, NJ 07090

Bergen County Genealogy Society Quarterly
16 Beech St.
Westwood, NJ 07675

Atlantic County Historical Society
907 Shore Rd.
P.O. Box 301
Somers Point, NJ 08244

Besides the Somers Mansion and Museum, this society houses over 1,000 books that are out of print, 3,500 personal papers, 125 manuscripts books, 100 Bibles including deeds, wills and diaries.

Loyalists records available:

Listed under the Boggs Family Papers, 1737-1942 (5 feet). New Jersey Loyalist Claims.

Listed under the William Nelson Papers, 1693-1914 (8 feet). Item 16, New Jersey Loyalists).

Andrew Bell Papers, 1742-1850 (3 feet). He was a Loyalist who kept a diary, was a secretary to Sir Henry Clinton, and later to Sir Guy Carleton.

Isaac Browne, Minister, sermons, 1736-76 (38 items). He favored the Loyalists.

Listed under the Nicolas Murray Papers, 1776-1846 (41 items). A list of local Loyalists.

Listed under James Parker, lawyer, journal, 1789-90 (1 volume). Trying to represent Sir Robert Barker in Greenwich to recover his lands lost because he was a Loyalist.

Listed under the Smith Family Papers, 1667-1960 (60 feet). Item #10, John Waddell, Loyalist papers.

Listed under the Essex County, New Jersey, clerks offices, book of warrants, 1784-87 (1 volume). Some Loyalist-forfeited estates.

Listed under the Jouet Family Papers, c. 1750-1890 (1 foot). The sermons of Rev. Cavalier Jouet, a Loyalist who fled to England and John H. Jouet of Nova Scotia.

The Genealogical Society of New Jersey
P.O. Box 1291
New Brunswick, NJ 08904

The Genealogical Society of Pennsylvania
1300 Locust St.
Philadelphia, PA 19107

Morris Area Genealogical Society
P.O. Box 105
Convent Station, NJ 07961-0105

The Genealogical Society of the Westfield
c/o Westfield Memorial Library
550 E. Broard St.
Westfield, NJ 07090

Bergen County Historical Society
Johnson Free Public Library
275 Moore St.
Hackensack, NJ 07601
Phone: 201-343-4169

Listed as subjects under their local history are Patriots and Loyalists.

New Jersey Taxation Records

Accelerated Indexing Systems published an index on these records from 1772 to 1822.

The Genealogical Magazine of New Jersey published some early tax lists starting at 1773.

The Revolutionary Census of New Jersey
By Kenn Stryker-Rodda. It is an index of tax ratables for 1773-74, 1778-80 and 1784-85.

Rutgers University

Archibald S. Alexander Library
169 College Ave.
New Brunswick, NJ 08901-1163
Phone: 732-932-7851
Fax #: 732-932-1101
Website: http://scc0l.rutgers.edu/alexhome/index.htm
Genealogy Department

This library has the best collections outside the state archives and library in Trenton. For the Loyalist period we have the following records which are owned by the Genealogical Society of New Jersey:

Loyalist Claims

Microfilm list of hundreds of Loyalists submitting claims for losses received during the war (Microfilm readers are available).

Family Records

Bible and family records, over 4,500.

John P. Dornan Collection, some Quaker information.

Charles H. Meeker Collection, on the family (cardex file).

Warren P. Coon Collection, 20,000 cards on family.

D. Staton Hammond Collection, cards on the family.

More Collections on Specific Families

Gulick, 24 notebooks.

Drake family.

Van Duyn family.

Selover family, 5 notebooks.

Bloomfield family.

James Murray Collection including the Hart family.

Charles Carroll Gardner Collection. Card file up to early 1800's and notes on New Jersey families through middle of 1700's.

Many other unpublished materials on various families.

Military Records

Chester N. Jones Collections. 30,000 cards on soldiers in the Revolutionary War.

Miscellaneous Records

Correspondence, diaries, account books, deeds, etc.

Tax Records

New Jersey Ratables, 1778-1822

New Jersey Tax Lists, 1772-1822

PENNSYLVANIA

This colony had a real problem at the outbreak of the Revolutionary War. Nearly one sixth of its population were religious objectors (mostly Quakers) to any type of warfare, and this was not counting the supporters of the British. Out of a population of nearly 250,000, that stood to be a pretty large number against the fight for independence from the Crown. Quaker records could be of some value here because they disowned members who took part in the war, and their records show this. Now, keep in mind that a marriage outside their faith and any wrongdoing of members would also bring on disowning. These records should be checked carefully.

In 1777, the British invaded Philadelphia and occupied it. The following institutions may be of value to you if you have Loyalists from Pennsylvania:

Pennsylvania State Archives

P.O. Box 1026
Harrisburg, PA 17108-1026
Phone: 717-783-3281
Website:
http://www.state.Pa.us/PA_Exec/Historical_museum/Dam/geniel.htm

There is a colonial record that consists of 138 volumes and must be examined with help of an index provided by the State Library of Pennsylvania, entitled "Guide to the Published Archives of Pennsylvania." This index is broken down into nine series, but series 2, 3, 5 and 6 pertain to the Revolutionary War records listing muster rolls, pay rolls, accounts, militia lists, pensions, land warrants and land donations.

Note: These are Patriot records, but you may find that your Loyalist deserted from these ranks.

Military Records

Over 100,000 cards on file of men who served in the Pennsylvania military. (The staff has made searches in these files for patrons). These relate to military service between 1775-1809.

Pennsylvania State Library

Walnut and Commonwealth Ave.
Harrisburg, PA 17101

This library holds many publications on the Revolutionary War and has an extensive genealogical section. Many of these works are from the D.A.R. materials. There are some out-of-state listings here too. Many books on military lists.

Contains over 5,000 printed genealogies. Over 360 drawers of 3" X 5" index cards.

Genealogical Society of Pennsylvania

1300 Locust St.
Philadelphia, PA 19107
(Located in same building with Pennsylvania Historical Society)

The manuscripts section is off limits to genealogists, but you can get special permission for projects. Many collections have been microfilmed and are available to the public. The *Guide to Manuscript Collections* shows which ones are on microfilm. They also have many military rolls listed in printed materials. Their strong point is southern Pennsylvania.

They have the original copies of the eighteenth-century Supreme Court records (45 volumes, no index).

Gilbert Cope Collection of genealogy on 2,500 people in Chester and Southeastern Pennsylvania and in New Jersey, arranged alphabetically in 90 volumes.

The Division of Public Records

Branch of the Pennsylvania Historical and Museum Commission
Harrisburg, PA 17101

Has official records exclusively, but especially military service records dated 1775-1861. (These records cannot be handled because they are so fragile, but a certificate can be bought for a small fee).

Microfilm on pre-1850 records of thirteen of the oldest eastern counties.

The Friends Historical Library

Swarthmore College
500 College Ave.
Swarthmore, PA 19081-1905
Phone: 610-328-8497
Fax #: 610-328-7329
E-mail: friends@swarthmore.edu
Website: http://www.swarthmore.edu/library/Friends/index.html

This is the best location for Quaker records in the country. They have the following:

Quaker meeting records (minutes).
Births
Burials
Marriages
Removals and membership records

They will not conduct a search for you. You can go there or hire a genealogist to do the work.

American Friends Service Committee Archives

1501 Cherry Street
Philadelphia, PA 19102
Phone: 215-241-7044
Fax #: 215-241-7275
E-mail: archives@afsc.org
Website: http://www.afsc.org

Other Pennsylvania Records

Wills, deeds and mortgages are located in each courthouse of the 67 counties.

Philadelphia records for the city and county have been merged and are located at the City Hall, 13th and Market Streets in Philadelphia.

The David Library of the American Revolution

River Rd. (Rt. 32)
P.O. Box 48
Washington Crossing, PA 18977
Phone: 215-493-6776

This privately endowed foundation is devoted to the study of the American Revolution. The library is open to the public. The following records and functions are there:

Sol Feinstone's collection of Revolutionary War manuscripts. Printed material consisting of several thousand books.

Pamphlets, periodicals and newspapers printed in America and Great Britain.

Microfilm collections of over 10,000 reels and adding to it weekly (consisting of seven million documents).

Note: All microfilm has been taken from the National Archives in Washington, D.C., the Public Records Office in Britain and other record centers there, including various Canadian and German records from their archives.

Other programs sponsored by the library are a Fellowship program, a Playwriting Award and audio-visual programs, including additional grants.

The following list is only a few of the many sources they carry:

Andre, John (1751-1780). Journal, 1777-1778. Film 383

Breadalbane Military Manuscripts, 1775-81. Muster rolls of British 40th Regiment of Foot. Film 385.

British Headquarters Papers, 1763-1852. Film 30.

Byles Family Papers, 1757-1837. Boston Loyalist Family. Film 386.

Canada. New Brunswick Museum. American Loyalist Muster Rolls. Film 271.

Canada. National Archives. American Loyalist Muster Rolls. Film 273.

Canada. National Archives. Ward Chipman Papers: Muster & Regiment Papers, 1776-1785. Film 272.

Dorchester, Guy Carleton, Baron (1724-1808) Papers (30 reels). Film 57.

Great Britain. Audit Office. Papers of American Loyalist Claims Commission 1780-1835 (154 reels). Film 264 and (32 reels) Film 263.

Great Britain. Treasury. Miscellaneous Documents Relating to Refugees 1780-1836 (American Loyalists). Film 414.

Great Britain. War Office. Certificates of Birth, Baptisms, Marriages, and Deaths, Loyal American and Canadian Corps. (Loyalists family records). Film 415.

Periodicals and Books for Pennsylvania Research

The publications of the Genealogical Society of Pennsylvania (renamed the *Pennsylvania Genealogical Magazine*). The first 15 volumes contain wills, vital records, Friends Meeting records, etc.

Pennsylvania Society Quarterly. Published in Washington, D.C. since 1912. 47 volumes of family records, locations for research in Pennsylvania, Bible records, etc.

Municipal Archives of the City and County of Philadelphia. By Charles E. Hughes Jr. and Allen Weinberg.

A State Divided.
By A. Chesney. Pub. by Ohio State University, 1921.

Pennsylvania Internet Locations

Archives and Manuscripts Repositories
Website: http://lcweb.loc.gov/coll/nucmc/pasites.htm
This site lists over 50 locations to search throughout Pennsylvania

FLORIDA

Florida played a part in the Loyalist chapter too. Many fled there while being pursued by the victorious Patriots. Since Florida was under Spanish rule until 1763, some Spaniards lived in and around the St. Augustine area where the Loyalists settled. But now Florida belonged to the British, and with the outbreak of the war and the fall of Charleston and Savannah, approximately 12,000 Loyalists fled to east Florida. The Georgians and Carolinians were not the only Loyalists to flee to Florida. Many from Virginia, Pennsylvania, Connecticut and Massachusetts came for shelter and protection, and by 1783 there was a very strong Loyalist community established in and around St. Augustine. When the war ended, their new home was once again uprooted with the control of the territory going back to Spain.

Many went to Providence Island in the Bahamas, and others to England. Some stayed and tried to live with the new Spanish rule, and others found their way back into the United States and Canada. The following numbers have been established:

462 whites and 2,561 blacks returned to the United States.
725 whites and 155 blacks went to Nova Scotia.
1,033 whites and 2,214 blacks went to the Bahamas.
421 whites and 1,156 blacks went to Jamaica, Dominica and other parts of the Caribbean.
246 whites and 35 blacks possibly went to England.
61 whites and 217 blacks went to other foreign countries.

The following locations and records may be of help for the Loyalist-hunter in Florida.

Florida State Archives

R.A. Gray Building
500 South Bronough St.
Tallahassee, FL 32399-0250
Website: telnet://stafla.dlis.state.fl.us:23

They have a fine collection of Revolutionary War records concerning troops from other states, D.A.R. records, and many from the lower southern colonies, too.

University of Florida

Library West
Gainsville, FL 32601
Website: http://www.lib.usf.edu/spccoll/

On file in the Microtext room, 3rd floor, are the American Loyalists Claims:

A.O. 12, Series 1
(Microfilm, 30 Reels)

A.O. 13, Series 2
(Microfilm, 145 Reels)

Note: Library call number: E 277 .G74

Presently, there are two volumes to these claims in print listing each name of the Loyalists, their location in the files, compiled by Clifford S. Dwyer.

Note: During the evacuation of Georgia from Savannah, many had to travel overland to St. Augustine, Florida.

Military Regiments

West Florida Foresters

Note: Found at the National Archives, Ontario, Canada, listed under Northern Canadian Division.

Florida Societies

The St. Augustine Historical Society
St. Augustine, FL 32084

West Florida Genealogical Society
P.O. Box 947
Pensacola, FL 33566

Note: Many other societies exist for research. You can contact one of the above for their address.

Florida Books & Material

East Florida as a British Province, 1763-1784. By Charles L. Mowat. Pub. by University of Florida Press, 1964.

The Loyalists in East Florida, 1774-1785. By Wilbur H. Siebert. Pub. by Florida State Historical Society, 1929, 2 volumes.

British St. Augustine. By Leitch J. Wright Jr. Pub. by Historic St. Augustine Preservation Board, 1975.

Florida in the America Revolution. Pub. by University of Florida Press, 1975. Author unknown.

Florida Internet Locations

Florida USGenWeb Page
Website: http://www.rootsweb.com/~flgenweb/index.html

Julia's Southern States Genealogy – Florida
Website:
http://www.geocities.com/Heartland/Meadows/5387/FLORIDA.HTML

GEORGIA

With only three thousand Patriots, this colony was one of the smallest involved in the war. Consisting of only eight eastern counties, and heavily dependent on the King and the British troops for support, they were not represented at the First Continental Congress in 1774. The first founders of Savannah, Georgia were Loyalists. A present-day mayor tried to turn down a recommendation to erect a memorial to the Loyalists, likening them to the Nazis. The town council saw the historical value of the memorial and overturned his veto.

After 1778, the British restored their rule in this colony with hundreds of men swearing allegiance to the King. But that was short-lived because they had to depart again in July 1782, with Tories remaining as long as they agreed to join the Georgia Continental Line for two years, or for the duration of the war. Thousands of others chose to leave and were given transport by the British. Many fled to St. Augustine, Florida, overland when no ships were available.

Georgia Department of Archives and History

Ben W. Fortson, Jr. Archives and Records Building
330 Capitol Ave., S.E.
Atlanta, GA 30334
Phone: 404-565-2393
Fax #: 404-657-8427
Website: http://www.sos.state.ga.us/archives/

Located in a brand-new building (1990), they have an extensive collection of genealogy. Admission cards are issued at first visit. A film is offered on the holdings in the library.

Many general works are on the shelves, especially many D.A.R. documents and books.

Societies in Georgia

Augusta Genealogical Society, Inc.
P.O. Box 3743
Augusta, GA 30914-3743
E-mail: (Jim Moore) jmoore@interoz.com

Georgia Genealogical Society
P.O. Box 54575
Atlanta, GA 30308-0575
E-mail: ggs@america.net

NORTH CAROLINA

This colony is credited with having the first royal governor to flee at the outbreak of the Revolution. Governor Josiah Martin left on 31 May 1775. There were hardly any British in North Carolina throughout the war. In 1781, Josiah Martin returned with Cornwallis and restored royal rule on October 3, but it did not last long after the defeat at King's Mountain to the south where many British and Loyalists died. Within weeks, the British were gone again. The following institutions are where material can be found:

North Carolina State Archives

Department of Cultural Resources
Division of Archives and History
109 East Jones St.
Raleigh, NC 27611-2807
Phone: 919-733-3952

Housed in the Archives and History Buildings, the North Carolina State Archives shares this structure with the state library. Here are stored the vouchers or certificates (notes) which number between 40,000 and 50,000. These were money notes, and when turned in, a hole was usually punched in them and a signature was required of the holder so they couldn't be used again. This source is only good for establishing your ancestor's location during the war period, and good for a record of his signature.

They also have Land Warrants and Proof of Military Service records, but these are for Patriots. They would offer hope of locating your Loyalist if he changed sides. Only one of two muster rolls survived and are published in vol. XVI of the State Records of North Carolina. They also have the county court records. Most are not indexed.

North Carolina State Library

109 East Jones St.
Raleigh, NC 27602

They have an extensive collection of Revolutionary War records, and the location compliments the archives. Holdings are various D.A.R. records and several other collections for other states, including *The King's Mountain Men* by Katherine White.

Loyalists Societies and Newsletters

The Society of Loyalists Descendants (Now closed down)
(A Branch of The Society for History, Research and Preservation, Inc.)
P.O. Box 484
Rockingham, NC 28379
Phone: 919-997-6641

The only single Loyalist (only) organization located in the United States, this was of very high quality, and their history branch can direct you or give you historical materials. The Loyalist part of the society was created to gather information and give help on Loyalist studies and research. Their purpose was to establish a proper view of both sides of the conflict.

Newsletter

They published a very high quality newsletter, the best outside the Loyalist Gazette in Canada. The materials consisted of Loyalist genealogies, stories, records, queries and ads about Loyalists. The Editor and founder was Joe M. McLaurin. I was very sadden to see this society come to an end.

Other North Carolina Societies and Libraries

Richmond County Historical Collection
P.O. Box 848
Rockingham, NC 28379
Phone: 919-997-6641
Director was and possibly still is, Joe M. McLaurin

Collection of over 200,000 documents and records on North Carolina.

North Carolina Genealogical Society
P.O. Box 1492
Raleigh, NC 27602
Phone: 919-733-3991

North Carolina Books on Loyalist

The Loyalists in North Carolina during the Revolution.
By O.R. DeMond. Pub. by Shoe String Press, 1963-64.

SOUTH CAROLINA

This colony was divided in half during the war, and many battles were fought here, including the famous battle at King's Mountain where mostly civilians fought with each other. When the Loyalists lost on 7 October 1780, they never regained control. In June 1776, the British fleet was beaten back, killing Lord Campbell on his ship. Four years later the British took the city back (as they did in the north). Internal fighting broke out and families divided turned the area into a bloodbath, affecting every section of the colony. On 14 December 1782, over 3,000 British troops from New York City evacuated Charleston, taking with them 3,800 Loyalists and 5,000 slaves. This finally ended the British rule in South Carolina.

South Carolina Department of Archives and History

Senate and Bull Streets
P.O. Box 11669
Columbia, SC 29211
Phone: 803-734-8577

The greatest holdings that this library has are the *Stub Entries to Indents Issued in Payment of Claims Against South Carolina Growing Out of the Revolution* (12 volumes). Because of the destruction of all the other records, these records are very important.

The book, *South Carolina Patriots in the American Revolution.* By Dr. Bobby Gilmore Moss, published by Genealogical Pub. Co., lists nearly 20,000 soldiers.

Revolutionary War Pension Files, 89 rolls is located here. It is in a set that was purchased from the National Archives.

Roster of Patriots at King's Mountain, microfilm reel of those who served there (box #F).

Various books and materials concerning troops, battles and genealogies.

University of South Carolina

South Carolina Library
Sumter Street near Pendleton St.
Columbia, SC 29202

Noted as being the nations first college library, it carries many publications regarding the Revolutionary War period, including D.A.R. records and various registers of troops from this state and others.

Other Loyalist Materials Pertaining to South Carolina

British Colonial Records, C.C. 305/82, fos. 597-600)at the Library of Congress, Wash. DC). This is a list of British sympathizers, Loyalists or Tories who were massacred in South Carolina.

Jacob Adams, Ephraim Malone and Benjamin Malone were some of the Loyalist settlers who started the colony in the Bahamas. They were from South Carolina.

VIRGINIA

This commonwealth was the most populated, with nearly 450,000 people, half of them slaves, but many were still very active against the British cause. It is said that almost 50,000 men served on the Patriot side, making this colony one of the toughest to control for the British. Representing over sixty regiments, this source of Patriot records may be useful to the Loyalist researcher whose ancestor deserted from their ranks. Keep in mind that West Virginia was part of Virginia at this time.

Census & Other Records

In case your Loyalist had property sold after the war or moved back down, the following may be useful.

Tax Lists from 1787.

1800 census for Accomack and Louisa counties are the only ones surviving the years.

Early Virginia Land Records: 1619 to 1921.

Survey Plats: 1779 to 1878

Land Grants: 1690 to 1862

Land Warrants: 1779 to 1926

Miscellaneous Land Records: 1779 to 1923

Virginia State Library & Archives Division

11th Street and Capitol Square
Richmond, VA 23219

Works consist of the D.A.R. records, and various other books (nearly 200), all Patriot in nature.

All births, deaths and marriages prior to 1896 are housed here too.

Library of Virginia

800 E. Broad Street
Richmond, VA 23219
Phone: 804-692-3500 (Main), 804-692-3777 (Lib. Ref), 804-692-3600 (Records)
Fax # 804-692-3556

Library of Virginia, Digital Collection Website: http://image.vtls.com/

Virginia Colonial Records Database on Internet: http://leo.vsla.edu/colonial/vcrp.html

Earl Gregg Swem Library

College of William and Mary
Williamsburg, VA 23187-8794

Societies in Virginia

Virginia Genealogical Society
5001 West Broad Street, Suite 115
Richmond, VA 23230-3023
Phone: 804-285-8954
Website: http://www.vgs.org/

Lower DelMarVa Genealogical Society
P.O. Box 3602
Salisbury, MD 21802-3602
Phone: 410-742-3501 or 410-546-0314
Website: http://bay.intercom.net/ldgs/index.html

Virginia Historical Society
428 North Boulevard
P.O. Box 7311
Richmond, VA 23221-0311
Phone: 804-358-4901
E-mail: kelly_winters@vahistorical.org
Website: http://www.vahistorical.org

Genealogy and History of the Eastern Shore (GHOTES)
Website: http://www.esva.net/ghotes/

Virginia GenWeb Project
Website: http://www.rootsweb.com/~vagenweb/

Order of Descendants of Ancient Planters
Website: http://tyner.simplenet.com/PLANTERS.HTM

Virginia Books & Materials

Loyalists in the Southern Campaign of the Revolutionary War. By Murtie June Clark. Pub. by Genealogical Pub. Co. This 3-volume set is the best source on the market for finding the Loyalists who served in the south. Thousands of names are listed.

Loyalism in Virginia
By Harrell. Pub. by Duke University, 1928.

Historical Register of Virginians in the Revolution, Soldiers, Sailors, Marines, 1775-1783, by John Hastings Gwathmey. Pub. by Dietz Press, Richmond, 1938.

Virginia Soldiers of 1776 (3 vols), by Louis A. Burgess. Pub. by Gene. Pub. Co., 1973 (Reprint from 1927-29). Listing over 35,000 soldiers.

Miscellaneous United States Archives Locations For Inquiries

Alabama
Department of Archives & History
624 Washington Ave.
Montgomery, AL 36130

Alaska
Alaska State Archives
141 Willoughby Ave., Pouch C
Juneau, AK 99811

Arizona
Arizona State Library
Dept. of Library, Archives & Public Records
State Capitol
1700 West Washington
Phoenix, AZ 85007

Arkansas
Arkansas History Commission
One Capitol Mall
Little Rock, AR 72201

California
California Secretary of State
California State Archives
1020 O Street, Room 138
Sacramento, CA 95814

Colorado
Colorado Department of Administration
Division of State Archives & Public Records
1313 Sherman St., 1-820
Denver, CO 80203

Hawaii
Hawaii Department of Accounting & General Services
Archives Division
Iolani Palace Grounds
Honolulu, HI 96813

Idaho
Idaho State Historical Society
Division of Manuscripts & Idaho State Archives
610 North Julia Davis Drive
Boise, ID 83702

Illinois
Illinois Office of the Secretary of State
Archives Division
Archives Building
Springfield, IL 62756

Indiana
Indiana State Library, Archives Division
1D0 North Senate Ave.
Indianapolis, IN 46204

Iowa
Iowa State Historical Society of Iowa
State Archives, Capitol Complex
Des Moines, IA 50319

Kansas
Kansas State Historical Society
120 West Tenth St.
Topeka, KS 66612

Kentucky
Kentucky Public Records Division
Archives Research Room
P.O. Box 537
Frankfort, KY 40602-0537

Louisiana
Louisiana Secretary of State
Archives & Records Division
P.O. Box 94125
Baton Rouge, LA 70804

Michigan
Michigan Department of State
Michigan History Division, State Archives Unit
717 West Allegan
Lansing, MI 48918

Minnesota
Minnesota Historical Society
Division of Archives & Manuscripts
1500 Mississippi Street
St. Paul, MN 55101

Mississippi
Mississippi Department of Archives & History
100 South State St.
P.O. Box 571
Jackson, MS 39205

Missouri
Director Records Management & Archives Service
Secretary of State's Office
P.O. Box 778
1001 Industrial Drive
Jefferson City, MO 65102

Montana
Montana Historical Society
Division of Archives & Manuscripts
225 North Roberts St.
Helena, MT 59601

Nebraska
Nebraska State Historical Society
State Archives Division
1500 R Street
Lincoln, NE 68508

Nevada
Nevada State Library & Archives
Division of Archives & Records
101 South Fall St.
Carson City, NV 89710

New Mexico
New Mexico State Records Center & Archives
Historical Services Division
404 Montezuma
Santa Fe, NM 87503

North Dakota
State Archives & Historical Research Library
North Dakota Heritage Center
Bismarck, ND 58505

Ohio
The Ohio Historical Society
Archives-Manuscripts Division
1985 Velma Ave.
Columbus, OH 43211

Oklahoma
Oklahoma Department of Libraries
Archives & Records Division
200 Northeast 18th St.
Oklahoma City, OK 73105

Oregon
Oregon Secretary of State
Archives Division
Oregon State Archives & Records Center
1005 Broadway, N.E.
Salem, OR 97310

South Dakota
South Dakota Department of Education & Cultural Affairs
South Dakota State Archives
State Library Building
800 Governors Dr.
Pierre, SD 57501-2294

Tennessee
Tennessee State Library & Archives
403 7th Avenue North
Nashville, TN 37219

Texas
Texas State Library
Archives Division
P.O. Box 12927
Austin, TX 78711

Utah
Utah State Archives & Records Service
State Capitol, Room B-4
Salt Lake City, UT 84114

Washington
Office of the Secretary of State
Division of Archives & Records Management
P.O. Box 9000
Olympia, WA 98504-9000

West Virginia
Department of Culture & History
Archives & History Division, Science & Cultural Center
Capitol Complex
Charleston, WV 25305

Wisconsin
State Historical Society of Wisconsin
Archives Division
816 State St.
Madison, WI 53706

Wyoming
Wyoming Archives, Museum & Historical Department
Archives & Records Management Division
Barrett Building
Cheyenne, WY 82002

4 *OTHER COUNTRIES LOYALIST SETTLED AT*

ENGLAND

London had a section settled by the American Loyalists, but was not very happy to take in these refugees. They were given a very hard time in hopes that many would return to America.

The Public Records Office

Ruskin Ave. Kew, Richmond, Surrey England TW9 4DU Phone: 010876-3444 (Main research location)	&	Chancery Lane London England WC2A 1LR Phone: 01-405-0741

They cannot do research for you, but will supply a list of researchers who charge a fee. The information in these records goes back as far as 1695.

The following is a list of guides that are available for research:

Guide to the Contents of the Public Records Office. Vols. 1 & 2. Pub. by the Public Records Office. A description of all the classes of records.

Public Records Office Handbook No. 3: The Records of the Colonial and Dominions Offices. Pub. by the Public Records Office. Outline of Colonial Office Records.

Guide to the Material for American History to 1783, in the Public Records Office of Great Britain. By C.M. Andrews. 2 vols. By the British Museum. Pub. by Kraus Reprint Corp., NY, 1965. This is a very good guide to these records.

A Guide to Manuscripts Relating to America in Great Britain & Ireland. By B.R. Crick & M. Alman. Pub. by Meckler Books, Westport, CT, 1979. A guide for Britain and Ireland archives records.

The British Public Records Office: History, Description, Record Groups, Finding Aids and Materials for American History, with special reference to the state of Virginia Library, Richmond, Virginia, 1960.

Claims for compensation for losses are located at The Public Records Office, London, England. This section is entitled, "Audit Office (A.O.) 12 and 13." Keep in mind that only a small portion of Loyalists had the resources to document their losses and to submit their claims to the Crown. Where a claim can be found, you may locate records stating the Loyalists former residence, income, what they did for a living, property values, some dependent information, and naturally, their military records. There is an index of these claims in volume 109, which also gives the decision of the claim.

Two volumes to The American Loyalists' Claims compiled by Clifford S. Dwyer were taken from the A.O. 12 series 1 and A.O. 13 series 2 records that were extracted from the Great Britain Public Records Office in London, England. This is an index and the works are on microfilm located at the Library West, University of Florida, Gainsville, FL. Pub. by RAM Pub., DeFuniak Springs, FL 32433, 1985.

Documents of the American Revolution, 1770-1783, by K.G. Davies. Pub. by Irish University Press, Shannon, Ireland, 1972. 21 volumes of calendars and transcripts.

Calendars of certain Colonial Office records published in *Report on Canadian Archives for 1890, 1894, and 1895.* Material relating to Quebec, Nova Scotia and Prince Edward Island.

American Loyalist Claims – Copies of Treasury Minutes.
Class: T.79/97/A. SR # SR03042. Reel # 283. Dates: 1777-1783. References lists and indexes XLVI, p.104. Loyalist losses 5 Aug. 1777 to 22 May 1783.

Loyalist Claims, Series II – Virginia Claims.
Class: A.C. 13/32. SR# SR02248. Reel # 254. Dates 1777-1789. References list and indexes XLVI, p.194

Loyalist Claims, Series I – Examinations on Fresh Claims, 1782-1783.
Class: A.O. 12/99. SR# SR03138. Reel # 267. Dates: 1783. References lists and indexes XLVI, p.193. Examines claims for losses sustained by Loyalists from Virginia and other colonies.

PRO L&I: XXVIII: List of War Office Records

Records of Loyalists who served with British Army in North America; returns, muster books, pay lists (WO 10, WO 12, and WO 13). Consult the Search Department at PRO, Kew. An alphabetical guide to war office and other military records. A computerized index list of Hessian troops.

Loyalist Regiment Rolls 1777-1783 are held at the National Archives in Ottawa, Ontario, Canada.

Many private papers, such as the Cornwallis, Gage and Chatham papers.

Societies in England

Society of Genealogists
37 Harrington Gardens
London, England SW7 4JX

Note: There are many societies located in every county. A list can be obtained from the above mentioned.

Books on Loyalists In England

The Flight of American Loyalists to the British Isles.
By Wilbur Siebert. Pub. by F.J. Herr Printing Co., 1911.

The British Americans: The Loyalist Exiles in England.
By Mary Beth Norton, Boston, 1972.

England Internet Connections

The Public Record Office (PRO)
Site Location: http://www.pro.gov.uk/
Genealogy Section: http://www.pro.gov.uk/readers/genealogists/default.htm.

Records Management – United Kingdom
Website: http://britac3.britac.ac.uk/rms/index.html

BAHAMAS

Many Loyalist refugees fled to the Bahamas and settled there, mostly at Hope Town, Marsh Harbour, Cherokee Sound, Green Turtle Cay, Great Guana Cay and Man-O-War Cay. Some descendants today have 100% Loyalist blood because of their close bond and lack of desire to interbreed with other areas located on other islands. Basically, they stayed in their own world. Carleton was settled September 1783 by mostly Loyalists from New York City, starting out with over 600 people. Many other Loyalists came from Florida after England ceded that territory back to Spain. Carleton slowly dispersed into other areas of the island, fading all hopes of making it into a commercial area for the Loyalists.

Hope Town, located at Elbow Cay in Abaco, was founded in 1785 by the Loyalists.

At New Plymouth, Bahamas, on 14 November 1987, a monument was erected honoring the Loyalist who settled the area. Twenty-four prominent Bahamians were descended from these Loyalists. Prime Minister Brian Mulroney of Canada paid tribute by presenting a memorial.

In 1983 an historical memorial was placed at Carleton Point near the site of the Loyalist settlement to commemorate the Loyalist founders in September 1783. Stating a short history of the settlement, its bronze plate is all that is left of that sandy area.

Today, archeologists are digging up the Loyalists' past, trying to piece together their lives in this beautiful tropical island.

Another account of how many Loyalists went to the Bahamas shows, 1,033 whites and 2,214 African Americans.

Historical Places and Societies

The Wyannie Malone Historical Museum
Hope Town, Bahamas

Records and artifacts can be found on the Loyalists. Also, records of Loyalists Graveyards.

Albert Lowe Museum
New Plymouth,
Abaco, Bahamas

Bahamas Archeological Project
Nassau, Bahamas

Bahamas Field Study Program of the College Center of the Finger Lakes, New York
San Salvador, Bahamas

Carleton Point Project
Abaco, Bahamas

Historical Association of Southern Florida
Miami, Florida

The Public Library
Rawson Square
Nassau, Bahama Islands

Military Regiments

Nassau Blues (records are at the National Archives in Ottawa, Ontario, Canada listed under Northern Canadian Division).

Bahamas Books & Records

Burial Grounds of Hope Town and Gravestone Inscriptions in Other Abaco, Bahamas Cemeteries. By Col. J.J. McAleer & Virginia W. McAleer. Pub. by The Berkshire Group 1987. This book lists all the graveyards, and the Loyalists and their descendants given in cemetery records.

Abaco, The History of an Out Island and its Cays. By Steve Dodge. Pub. by White Sound Press, Ill. One chapter is devoted to the American Loyalists.

The Early Settlers of the Bahama Islands. By Talbot A. Bethell. Pub. by Norfolk, England (updated).

Homeward Bound: A History of the Bahamas Islands to 1850, With a Definitive Study of Abaco in the American Loyalist Plantation Period. By Sandra Riley. Pub. by Miami Island Research, 1983.

Bahamian Loyalists and Their Slaves. By Gail Saunders. Pub. by MacMillan Caribbean, 1983

Note: The United Empire Loyalists' Association of Canada has recorded that the following countries also took in some Loyalists. Of the total population that settled in these countries, in some cases, the number of Loyalists is not known.

BERMUDA

Bermuda Societies

The small Island of Bermuda has an interesting relationship between Britain and the United States. In 1775, Bermuda sent a small delegation to the Continental Congress in Philadelphia looking into joining the rebellion. It is not known at this time why the change of heart occurred, but there was an incident while under British rule. Bermuda had large reserves of gunpowder, and George Washington needed it. On the other hand, the Bermudians needed food, so they broke into the powder magazine at Fort William. During the night they took 100 barrels of gunpowder out of the fort to Tobacco Cove where several ships were waiting. The deed was very much welcomed and Congress approved a large rationing of food to be sent to Bermuda, one to last the entire year. The special relationship between America and Bermuda lasted throughout the Revolutionary War After the war, their relationship with Britain grew closer, and by 1812 British ships sailed from Bermuda to help take Washington D.C., and burn the White House down.

Bermuda Historical Society
c/o Bermuda Library
Par-la-villa Park
Hamilton, Bermuda

St. George Historical Society
St. George, Bermuda

Miscellaneous Researchers

Mark & Deborah Petrie
Website: mpetrie@mail.island.net
They are looking for and studying American Loyalists in Bermuda.

SIERRA LEONE

Most of the Loyalists that went here were from Nova Scotia and left there around 1790. Their treatment in Nova Scotia was poor because they were all African/Americans. They sought freedom in Sierra Leone, Africa, but their plight was worse. After getting approval to leave and a few ships to take them there, disease and starvation nearly wiped out the entire colony.

JAMAICA

No information available except that many came from Florida. That total count to the Caribbean area was 421 whites and 1,156 African Americans.

DOMINICA

No information available except that many came from Florida. That total count to the Caribbean area was 421 whites and 1,156 African Americans

ISLANDS OF ST. VINCENT

No information available except that many came from Florida. That total count to the Caribbean area was 421 whites and 1,156 African Americans

5 *LOYALIST BOOK PUBLISHERS & BOOKS*

Besides the many other books scattered throughout this guide, below are listed more publications and publishers on the subject. My apologies to those missed

Book Publishers

Picton Press
P.O. Box 250
Rockport, ME 04856-0250
Phone: 207-236-6565
Fax: 207-236-6713

Generation Press
172 King Henry's Blvd., Agincourt, Ontario, Canada M1T 2V6

Mika Publishing Company
200 Stanley St.
P.O. Box 536
Belleville, Ontario
Canada K8N 5B2

Dundrun Press LTD
P.O. Box 245, Station F
Toronto, Ontario
Canada M4Y 2L5
Phone: 416-368-9390

Heritage Books Inc.
1540E Pointer Ridge Place
Bowie, MD 20716
Phone: 301-390-7709

Genealogical Publishing Co.
Baltimore, MD

New Ireland Press
Box 905 Station A
Fredericton, New Brunswick
Canada E3B 5B4

Miscellaneous Loyalist Books & Materials

The Nature of American Loyalism: Proceedings of the American Antiquarian Society, by Leonard W. Labaree, LIV, 1944.

While The Women Also Wept
By Janice Potter McKinnon (date & publisher unknown).

The Burning of the Valleys
By Gavin K. Watt (date & publisher unknown).

Loyalist Mosaic: A Multi-ethnic Heritage
By Joan Magee. Pub. by Dundurn Press, 1984

Eleven Exiles: Accounts of Loyalists
By Phyllis R. Blakeley & John N. Grant. Pub. by Dundurn Press, 1982

The Loyalists: Revolution, Exile, Settlement
By Christopher Moore. Pub. by Macmillan of Canada, 1984

A Dutch Heritage
By Joan Magee. Pub. by Dundurn Press, 1983.

The Loyalist Americans
By Robert S. Allen. Pub. by National War Museum of Canada, 1983. Printed by Alger Press.

Biographical Sketches of Loyalists of the American Revolution
By Gregory Palmer. Pub. by Meckler Pub. Co., 11 Ferry Lane, West Westport, CT 05808.

The Bibliography of Loyalist Source Materials in Archives in the United States, Canada and Great Britain. Westport, CT, 1981.

American Loyalist Claims
By Peter Coldham. Pub. by the National Genealogical Society, 1980.

American Vital Records From The Gentlemen's Magazine 1731-1868.
Compiled by Sylvanus Urban and David Dodson. Pub. by Genealogical Pub. Co., 1987.

Lieutenant Colonel George Campbell, King's American Regiment.
By Colin Campbell. Twelve pages of written material taken from an English journal (pages 306-316) and published privately by the author.

Loyalists of the American Revolution.
By Lorenzo Sabine. Pub. by Genealogical Pub. Co., 1979, 2 volumes. Reprinted from 1864 2nd Edition.

Loyalists And Red Coats.
By R.H. Smith. Pub. by University of North Carolina Press, 1965-66.

Orderly Book of the Three Battalions of Loyalists Commanded by Brigadier – General Oliver DeLancey 1776-1778.
Compiled by W. Kelby. Pub. by New York Historical Society, 1928.

United Empire Loyalists.
By J.T. Waugh. Pub. by University of Buffalo, Buffalo, NY, 1928.

Letters of a Loyalist Lady.
By A Hulton. Pub. by Harvard University Press, 1927.

A Divided People.
By Kenneth S. Lynn, Westport, CT, 1977.

Divided Loyalties.
By L.D. Enistein. Pub. by Houghton, 1933.

Loyalist Inhabitants.
By J.W. Chalmers. Pub. by The Institute of Applied Art, 1938.

Loyalists.
By J.F. Barrett. Pub. by Kenedy, 1943.

The American Tory
By William H. Nelson, Oxford, 1961.

Traitor.
By J. Fritz. Pub. by Puffin Books, 1989. A biography for young people.

The Loyalists in the American Revolution.
By C.H. Van Tyne. Pub. by Heritage Books Inc., MD, 1989.

A State Divided.
(Pennsylvania). By A.M. Ousterhout. Pub. by Greenwood Press, 1987.

Kentucky's Struggle with Its Loyalist Proprietors.
By W.H. Siebert. Pub. by author through the Ohio State University, 1920.

The Loyalists – The Story of Those Americans Who Fought Against Independence
By Donald Barr Chidsey (date and publisher unknown).

The American Loyalist: Origins and Nominal Lists.
By Diane Snyder Ptak. Pub. by D.S. Ptak, Albany, NY, 1993.

Loyalist Literature: An Annotated Bibliographic Guide to the Writings on the Loyalists of the American Revolution.
By Robert S. Allen. Pub. by Dundurn Press, Toronto, 1982.

Uses and Abuses of the American Loyalists' Claims
A Critique of Quantitative Analysis.
Pub. in the *William and Mary Quarterly Magazine*, 3rd Series, XXIV, 1968.

A Study of American Loyalism in Relation to British Colonial Government.
By Lawrence H. Gipson, Jared Ingersoll, New Haven, 1920.

6 *Laws & General Miscellaneous Loyalist Notations*

The Godfrey-Milliken Bill

MP John Godfrey and MP Peter Milliken, both Loyalist descendants, introduced a bill to the House of Commons in Canada on 24 July 1996 after the United States presented a bill by Senators, Helms-Burton which was passed letting people seek restitution from confiscated property from Cuba. The Godfrey-Milliken Bill would permit descendants of the United Empire Loyalists who fled the United States after the Revolutionary War to reclaim losses from confiscated property which was done unjustly and illegally by the American government according to the Treaty of Paris of 1783 which was an agreement between Britain and America after the war.

CBS, 60 Minutes aired this news development and it was also covered in the New York Times, Washington Post, Wall Street Journal and Times of London, as well as all throughout Canada. Today, there are roughly 3 million descendants from the approximate 80,000 Loyalists. Some people have already laid claim to sections of Manhattan, Washington DC, Philadelphia, Boston, Virginia and North Carolina.

The interesting thing about this story is that the United States ratified these rights by the US Congress, provided in Article V for: "the restitution of all Estates, Rights, and Properties, which have been confiscated."

American Indian Loyalist - Joseph Brant's Volunteers

Joseph Brant, also called Thayendanegea was a full-blooded Mohawk Indian who received a commission as Captain in the British Army. Most of his volunteers were from New York and its frontier. They received no pay, and they wore no uniforms. Their only distinction was a yellow piece of lace affixed to the headpiece. They were supplied from Fort Niagara. They settled mostly in Ontario after the war. There is a re-enactment organization of this unit today and the following person can be contacted for membership and more information:

David Broadhurst, Commander
54 Midway Drive
Bethel, CT 06801-2230
Phone: 203-798-2198

Lord Dorchester's Proclamation

On 9 November 1789, Lord Dorchester, the governor of Quebec declared and gave the right and honor to the families who had adhered to the "Unity of the Empire" the right to put the mark of honor after their surname.

"Those Loyalists who have adhered to the Unity of the Empire, and joined the Royal Standard before the Treaty of Separation in the year 1783, and all their children and their descendants by either sex, are to be distinguished by the following capitals, affixed to their names: U.E. Alluding to their great principal The Unity of the Empire.

Today, the United Empire Loyalists Association of Canada uses these capitals to award their members after proven descent. In 1979, Prince Philip came to Lennoxville, Quebec to celebrate the 200th Anniversary of this proclamation. Many Loyalist descendants, including this author were honored to meet his majesty.

Notable Dates In Loyalist History

18 May 1783, Spring Fleet landing at Saint John, New Brunswick.

19 May 1776, Nineteen days of flight of Sir John Johnson and company through the Adirondack Mountains to Montreal, Quebec.

22 May 1784, Mohawks landed at Tyendinaga, the first Loyalists at Bay of Quinte.

16 June 1784, Landing of Peter VanAlstine and Loyalists at Adolphustown, Ontario

19 June 1776, Formation of Sir John Johnson's 1st Kings Royal Regiment of New York.

24 June 1784, Disbandment of Loyalist Troops at Upper Posts.

19 July 1781, The Defense of the Blockhouse in Bergen Wood, New Jersey.

30 July 1783, Landing of 2nd Battalion, Kings Royal Regiment of New York at Cataraqui to rebuild Fort Frontenac, Quebec and prepared for arrival of Loyalists.

6 August 1777, Battle of Oriskany, on the Mohawk River.

16 August 1777, The Battle of Bennington, Vermont.

6 Sept. 1781, The burning of New London and massacre at Fort Griswold, Connecticut by Brig. General Benedict Arnold.

15 Sept. 1777, The formation of Butlers Rangers.

18 Sept. 1777, The first battle of Freeman's Farm near Saratoga.

20 Sept. 1783, Official end of hostilities in the American Revolution.

16 Oct. 1777, The Capitulation of General Burgoyne at Saratoga.

4 Nov. 1776, Loyalists join the British fleet at Crown Point.

12 June 1784, Royal approval of first settlement west of Ottawa Valley.

19 June, declared Loyalist Day in Ontario. Bill #150 for Province of Ontario, received 19 Dec. 1997.

24 Dec. 1783, Loyalists disbanded at Lower Canada.

31 Dec. 1775, American defeat and death of General Montgomery at walls of Quebec City.

7 *MISCELLANEOUS LOYALIST INTERNET SOURCES & LOCATIONS*

The Olive Tree Genealogy
By Lorine McGinnis Schulze
Has some Loyalist material
http://www.rootsweb.com/~ote/index.html

Loyalist, British Songs & Poetry of the American Revolution
http://www.erols.com/cadidus/music.htm

The Enigma of Benedict Arnold
By James Henretta.
A historical and military career outline of the famed Patriot/Tory/Traitor Benedict Arnold and how he was a hero on both sides of the American Revolution.
Http://www.earlyAmerica.com/review/Fall97/Arnold.html

Cyndi's List – Loyalists
Lists all kinds of Loyalist materials and locations on the net.
http://www.ctndislist.com/Loyalist.htm

Kings Rangers
A history and listing of the Kings Rangers, plus re-enactment organizations of today.
http://www.erols.com/candidus/kings.htm

Butlers Rangers
A history and listing of the Butlers Rangers, plus re-enactment organizations of today.
http://iaw.on.ca/~awoolleg/brang/brang.html

Maryland Loyalism & the American Revolution
This site is devoted to a book covering Maryland Loyalists, including regiment history.
http://www.erols.com/candidus/index.htm

Australian Records Management RFP
(Many Loyalist descendants relocated to Australia)
Website: http://www.ogit.gov.au/rational.html#RecordsManagement

Archives (Miscellaneous)
Website: http://mypage.direct.ca/d/dmattiso/

State Archives
Website: http://tls.unc.edu/archives/archive7.html

Other Heritage Books by the author:

Cemetery Inscriptions of the Town of Barnstable, Massachusetts, and Its Villages, 1600-1900

Cemetery Inscriptions of the Town of Barnstable, Massachusetts, and Its Villages, 1600-1900, with Corrections and Additions

French and Native North American Marriages, 1600-1800

Life of a Haunted House—The Barnstable House of Barnstable, Massachusetts: Genealogy of a Real Haunted House

Research Guide to Loyalist Ancestors: A Directory to Archives, Manuscripts, and Published Sources

Research Guide to Loyalist Ancestors: A Directory to Archives, Manuscripts, Published and Electronic Sources (Updated and Revised)

The House of Robinson—The Robinsons of Rhode Island: Their Genealogy and Letters, and the History of the Robinson & Son Oil Company of Baltimore, Maryland

The New Loyalist Index, Volume I

The New Loyalist Index, Volume II

The New Loyalist Index, Volume III: Including Cape Cod and Islands, Massachusetts, New Hampshire, New Jersey and New York Loyalists

Thunder Over New England—Benjamin Bonnell, the Loyalist: A Loyalist Story and Family Genealogy Including Other Loyalist Bunnell/Bonnell Genealogies

www.ingramcontent.com/pod-product-compliance
Lightning Source LLC
LaVergne TN
LVHW050644100826
845148LV00011B/1980